Logotherapy

Logotherapy

Viktor Frankl, Life and Work

Neil A. Soggie

ROWMAN & LITTLEFIELD
Lanham • Boulder • New York • London

Published by Rowman & Littlefield
A wholly owned subsidiary of The Rowman & Littlefield Publishing Group, Inc.
4501 Forbes Boulevard, Suite 200, Lanham, Maryland 20706
www.rowman.com

Unit A, Whitacre Mews, 26-34 Stannary Street, London SE11 4AB

British Library Cataloguing in Publication Information Available

Library of Congress Cataloging-in-Publication Data
Names: Soggie, Neil A. (Neil Alan) author.
Title: Logotherapy : Viktor Frankl, life and work / Neil A. Soggie.
Description: Lanham : Rowman & Littlefield, [2016] | Includes bibliographical references and index.
Identifiers: LCCN 2016023511 (print) | LCCN 2016029945 (ebook) | ISBN 9781442252080 (cloth : alk. paper) | ISBN 9781442252097 (Electronic)
Subjects: LCSH: Frankl, Viktor E. (Viktor Emil), 1905-1997. | Logotherapy. | Existentialism.
Classification: LCC RC489.L6 S64 2016 (print) | LCC RC489.L6 (ebook) | DDC 616.89/14—dc23
LC record available at https://lccn.loc.gov/2016023511

∞™ The paper used in this publication meets the minimum requirements of American National Standard for Information Sciences—Permanence of Paper for Printed Library Materials, ANSI/NISO Z39.48-1992.

Printed in the United States of America

Logotherapy

Viktor Frankl, Life and Work

Neil A. Soggie

ROWMAN & LITTLEFIELD
Lanham • Boulder • New York • London

Published by Rowman & Littlefield
A wholly owned subsidiary of The Rowman & Littlefield Publishing Group, Inc.
4501 Forbes Boulevard, Suite 200, Lanham, Maryland 20706
www.rowman.com

Unit A, Whitacre Mews, 26-34 Stannary Street, London SE11 4AB

British Library Cataloguing in Publication Information Available

Library of Congress Cataloging-in-Publication Data
Names: Soggie, Neil A. (Neil Alan) author.
Title: Logotherapy : Viktor Frankl, life and work / Neil A. Soggie.
Description: Lanham : Rowman & Littlefield, [2016] | Includes bibliographical references and index.
Identifiers: LCCN 2016023511 (print) | LCCN 2016029945 (ebook) | ISBN 9781442252080 (cloth : alk. paper) | ISBN 9781442252097 (Electronic)
Subjects: LCSH: Frankl, Viktor E. (Viktor Emil), 1905-1997. | Logotherapy. | Existentialism.
Classification: LCC RC489.L6 S64 2016 (print) | LCC RC489.L6 (ebook) | DDC 616.89/14—dc23
LC record available at https://lccn.loc.gov/2016023511

∞™ The paper used in this publication meets the minimum requirements of American National Standard for Information Sciences—Permanence of Paper for Printed Library Materials, ANSI/NISO Z39.48-1992.

Printed in the United States of America

Dedicated to Jordan, Emily, and Ayden

JOHN 1:1

Ἐν ἀρχῇ ἦν ὁ λόγος, καὶ ὁ λόγος ἦν πρὸς τὸν θεόν, καὶ θεὸς ἦν ὁ λόγος.
In the beginning was the Logos, and the Logos was with God, and the Logos was God.

The Greek New Testament – Fourth Edition Revised,

United Bible Societies, 1998.

Contents

Contents

Foreword

I hope you enjoy exploring the life and ideas of Viktor Emil Frankl as much as I do. It is my privilege to share with you his influence and legacy as the founder of the Third Viennese School of Psychotherapy.[1] Chapter 1 will give you a brief introduction of the early and middle years of Frankl's life.[2] Knowing his story will help you better understand his psychotherapeutic approach, known as *Logotherapy*.

May your meaning reveal itself through Viktor's life.

Neil A. Soggie

NOTES

1. Viktor E. Frankl, *Recollections: An Autobiography* (Cambridge, MA: Basic Books, 2000), 61.
2. Frankl, *Recollections*, 19–132.

Chapter 1

Viktor Frankl's Early Years

1905–1942

When people think of Viktor Frankl, they often conjure up emotions of terror, fear, despair, and the dark images of Nazi concentration camps. While people associate these images with Frankl's most famous book, *Man's Search for Meaning*, they do not typify the full life of the man himself. The life of Viktor Frankl is full of stories of humor, joy, and a wonderful sense of security that frames the context of his life. To understand Viktor Frankl, one must begin with the core emotional experience of his life, namely, joy.

As one of his earliest memories lays bare, Viktor was a young child on vacation with his family. On a particular summer morning, Viktor awoke to sensations of a warm breeze and birds chirping in the distance. With his eyes still shut, he emerged into a wakefulness of rapturous safety and security in love. As he opened his eyes, he saw the smiling face of his father over him; and he felt safe and loved.[1] These early core experiences and memories remained with Viktor throughout his life, giving him strength to face incredible challenges.

The Viktor Frankl story began in 1905 in Vienna, Austria: an age of prosperity, hope, and dreams. During this time Vienna was the seat of the Austro-Hungarian Empire, a bastion of Germanic political power. It was a large vibrant metropolis surrounded by picturesque mountains and beautiful forests. Vienna teemed with modern technology; yet, it held its atmosphere of culture, tradition, beauty, and charm. The region where the Frankls lived was near a public park and coffee shops where Viktor's parents were fond of visiting. According to Viktor, *Cafe Siller*,[2] on the edge of a park near their flat, was where his mother first felt the labor pains of his birth. "Little Vicky"[3] arrived to the family, two years behind his older brother Walter.

Viktor was proud of his family's flat at door 25, on the top floor of *Czerningasse* 6. He always thought it interesting that Dr. Alfred Adler had lived for a time, at number 7, diagonally across the street from the Frankls. Thus, Viktor would reflect, the birth of the Third Viennese School of Psychotherapy – *Logotherapy* – took place near that of the Second Viennese School, Dr. Adler's *Individual Psychology*. The first school, of course, was Sigmund Freud's *Psychoanalysis*.[4]

Viktor Frankl remained close to his parents throughout his life. He always recognized that he drew much of his personal characteristics from both his mother and father, especially when it came to his basic character. He saw his personality as a summation of his positive bonds with his parents. His father, Gabriel, was a stoic but occasionally hot-tempered man, personifying justice and love to his family. In these ways, Viktor believed that he took after his father, and even claimed that a Rorschach inkblot test he took at an Innsbruck psychiatric clinic confirmed this. What he inherited from his mother, he thought, was a deep wellspring of emotion that he could tap into in times of trial.[5]

Viktor believed in caring for family, and even during his childhood he lived this out – at the height of the First World War. Among the stories that he would tell, he recalled standing in a line at 3 a.m., in winter, to buy potatoes.[6]

Within school, he was a seeker of knowledge, interested in philosophers and in experimental pursuits. Viktor and his father went for walks through the university district and Gabriel would tell young Viktor stories of his own time in medical school. These walks likely helped to merge the philosopher/medical doctor identity of young Viktor. In his teen years, Viktor sought out wisdom for its own sake, apart from academic achievement.

Fascinated with the philosophical works of Wilhelm Ostwald and the psychological ideas of Theodor Fechner, he recalled making personal notes about the ways they work in the world. Young Viktor would experiment with both science and philosophy, in his search to understand the universe. As he advanced in school, he began taking adult evening classes in applied psychology and would bring the lessons learned back to his school classroom for demonstrations.[7]

As a teenager Viktor often went down the street to Prater Park, with his brother Walter and his younger sister Stella. The park became his intellectual playground. He often went there alone to think and make notes. When he went there with friends, he engaged them in discussions about philosophy, the new and intriguing field of psychology, and his long-held interest in medicine. He also began a bold time of writing to Sigmund Freud, and it was thrilling when Freud replied thoughtfully to each letter. Sadly, years later the Gestapo confiscated these valuable letters, and he lost these treasures.[8]

Viktor recalled times when his friends would simply roam through Prater Park, getting lost in their philosophical discussions and staying out most of the night. They were not getting into trouble or causing mischief like teenage boys are prone to do. Instead, they discussed Marx and Lenin, Freud, and Adler.[9]

One especially proud moment for Viktor came when he wrote an article in the park, about the origin of the mimic movements of affirmation and negation. As a bold teenager, Viktor quickly sent it off to Freud, hoping to please him with the work. The thrilling response from Freud was he sent the article for consideration in the *International Journal of Psychoanalysis.*[10]

For Viktor, his teen years were a time full of philosophical struggle. Though the battle was great, he never abandoned the challenges his own mind presented in living life. As he sought to understand his own existence, he eventually realized tensions are an important part of life. From these internal struggles, the embryonic ideas of Logotherapy were beginning to form. He was always enthusiastic about psychiatry, psychology, and psychoanalysis. His fascination with philosophy meant that he was giving lectures on the meaning of life at the age of 15. In these lectures he developed the idea we should not ask for the meaning of life; rather, life is asking us this question, "What is the meaning of this life?" It is we ourselves who must answer the existential question that life poses to us in everyday living. Our response comes in two ways: first, in our mindfulness of our experiences; second, in our choices to be responsible. A major task in life is to discover meaning.

Another basic truth that teenage Viktor discovered was the notion of ultimate meaning. The full meaning of a person's existence is beyond the grasp of human understanding. There exists *suprameaning*, but it isn't something supernatural. It is natural, simply a meaning beyond human grasp. This basic truth stresses that spirituality will be part of the genuine human life.[11]

Other children played out their fantasies of being soldiers, pirates, or a ship's captain. Young Viktor dreamed of becoming a doctor. His play up to and in his teen years centered on the identity of being a medical doctor. With the growing popularity of Freud and his theories, young Frankl became increasingly interested in the medical specialty of psychiatry. Finally, at the age of 19, Viktor made two giant leaps toward his eventual greatness. The first was his admittance into medical school. The second, perhaps a little more bold, was his application to join Sigmund Freud's Vienna Psychoanalytic Society. These early experiences, struggles, and goals set the stage for what was to become Viktor's most productive period.

As Viktor began to move through medical school at the University of Vienna, he struggled with choosing a specialization, first toying with the idea of going into either obstetrics or dermatology. However, a friend convinced Viktor that he had a different calling. Viktor's friend quoted from the philosopher Soren Kierkegaard to make his point: "Do not despair at wanting to become your authentic self."

That statement sparked Viktor to make a vital choice in his life, one that would affect everything that followed. Reflecting back, he marveled, "It is difficult to believe what decisive turns in our lives we sometimes owe to even casual remarks made by another person . . . from that moment on I made up my mind that I would no longer avoid my psychiatric self-actualization."[12]

With his training path chosen, he immersed himself in psychoanalysis but was disappointed by its reductionism. He felt that the psychoanalytic view did not satisfy his longing to understand people. He found himself drawn increasingly to Alfred Alder's *Individual Psychology*. Through Adler's group, as well as in his medical school studies, Viktor was able to explore other key research areas like psychosomatic medicine with mentors Drs. Rudolf Allers and Oswald Schwarz. "In 1927. . . . I had come under the spell of two men who impressed me not only as persons, but who also had a lasting influence on me through their ideas."[13]

Although a busy student, Viktor did find time to be active within the *Adlerian Society*. During this time he experienced the same concerns with Adler's view that he had previously with Freud's. In time, Viktor's mentors came to agree that Adler was too reductionistic and expressed their concerns openly at a meeting where Adler was present. Viktor was expelled from the society, despite his conciliatory position.

Allers and Schwarz had taken a decision to publicly withdraw from Alfred Adler's *Society of Individual Psychology* during a large meeting at the University of Vienna in 1927. During the meeting Adler was especially sensitive because he knew Freudians were present. When Allers and Schwarz announced their withdrawal over the concerns with Adler's perspective, Viktor too spoke up. Viktor tried to be appeasing, suggesting there was no reason to leave Adler's Society. Adler was upset by this treachery, especially in front of the Freudian psychoanalysts. Adler immediately broke all contacts with the three. In later years, Viktor tried to speak to him in a more casual setting, but Adler refused to reply: "He could not get over the fact that I had not supported him unconditionally."[14]

Following his expulsion from Adler's Society, Viktor took a brief break from theoretical pursuits and began focusing on practice. He did this through aiding in opening several student counseling centers and giving talks to groups of students. This transition time allowed him to incubate his own theory of meaning: "As early as 1929 I had developed the concept of three groups of values, or three possible ways to find meaning in life, for example: (1) A deed we do . . . (2) An experience we have . . . (3) An attitude we adopt. . . .."[15] Teaching classes also gave him an opportunity to meet women, which he found to be a pleasant side-benefit. Viktor used the occasion of a lecture to lure a woman that he had met at a dance. He would speak about this fantastic lecturer named Frankl, who gave the most fascinating lectures. He invited the woman to the lecture hall, where he saved a place near the front of the class for her. On settling into her seat, he sprung a surprise on her: "One can imagine the impression it would make on the girl as her date suddenly left his seat and, greeted with audience applause, step up to the lectern."[16]

After graduating from medical school in 1930, Viktor went on to specialize in general psychiatry and neurology. On completing his internships, he began a residency at Steinhof Psychiatric Hospital. During this residency period, Viktor was responsible for the treatment of severely depressed individuals, mostly suicidal women. It was here that he found great value in using his sense of humor in therapy. Here he pioneered the technique of *paradoxical intention*, a technique that he found useful in everyday situations. For example, he was stopped for a traffic violation and repeatedly told the officer how much he deserved the ticket. He went rambling on about how being written a ticket was well deserved. The officer reacted by calming Viktor down and not writing him a ticket.[17]

In the late 1930s, the Nazi influence was growing within Austria. This led some prominent individuals to worry about the future of Vienna. Initially the Jewish population of Vienna was hopeful. Sigmund Freud wrote to a friend that Austria "will not reach the height of brutality they have in Germany. . . . At present our government, upright and brave in its way, is more energetic in fending off the Nazi than ever before."[18]

In 1937 Viktor completed his residency and began a short-lived private practice. Politically, Nazi influence rose as Hitler put pressure on the Austrian government. The people of Vienna were on edge as they worried about Nazi extremism. Reflecting the times, Viktor's public lecture entitled *Nervousness as a Phenomenon of Our Time* was his reaction to the Nazi crisis:

> Suddenly the door was flung open, and an SA man stood there in Nazi uniform. Could something like that happen under our Chancellor Schuschnigg? I asked myself. Obviously the SA man intended to disturb the event and force an end to my lecture.
>
> I thought to myself, "I should make the impossible possible, and lecture in such a way that he will forget why he came here. Divert his attention!" So I faced him openly and kept on speaking. He remained at the doorway, not budging from his spot, until I had finished my lecture. This was the act of "rhetorical bravery" of my life![19]

When the Nazi influence finally began to dominate in the spring of 1938, it surprised the optimistic tone of Sigmund Freud and the hopeful nature of Viktor. Despite Freud's early hopefulness that the Nazi threat would pass Vienna by, eventually Freud, Adler, and many thousands of Jews in Vienna emigrated. The Nazis encouraged this emigration, and by late 1939, over half of the Jews in Vienna had left for other, presumably safer, places. The rest stayed in the city, hoping that they could hold on to their homes, loved ones, and possessions, despite the increasingly hostile climate.[20]

By late 1938 the anti-Semitic sentiment in Austria had reached a fever pitch, with the Nazi takeover of all Jewish establishments. Stripped of credentials, Jewish professionals had to wear a six-pointed yellow star, identifying themselves as Jews. This meant that Viktor was no longer able to run his private practice as a Jew. He soon received the post of chief of neurology at a Jewish hospital, Rothschild. It was his hope that this position would offer him and his aging parents a measure of protection from deportation.[21]

The Nazi's required all doctors in mental hospitals to identify those with a psychotic disorder or developmental disability. These patients were slated for euthanasia. While the euthanasia program was in effect, Viktor made an effort to save as many lives as possible. He found, at a Jewish home for senior citizens, a few beds set aside for those with psychotic disorders. He saved lives by certifying patients with schizophrenia as having other disorders, saving them from euthanasia. In this way, Viktor sought to evade the Gestapo enforced strict compliance with the law.

In September 1939, Germany invaded Poland, prompting France and Britain to declare war on Germany. During this time Viktor was the only sibling of the Frankl family who remained in Vienna, caring for and living with his parents, supporting them with whatever he could in hard times. Fortunately Viktor's position at Rothschild offered some protection from deportation to the concentration camps for both him and his parents, when deportations were increasing. The Nazis recognized a need for certain professions and allowed special privileges to those who filled the roles.[22]

In 1940 public pressure ended the Nazi euthanasia program in hospitals. The program left Viktor with a deep sense of fragility of life. Indeed, he did recall with sadness a few times when he could not save people. On one occasion, he picked up a Jewish husband and wife who could no longer remain in private care. Viktor noticed the taxi carrying the woman made a different turn than the taxi carrying the man. He asked the social worker with him, and the news shocked him. The wife had converted to Christianity; being no longer Jewish, she was not going to the Jewish Community Center. Instead, the social worker sent her to a mental hospital and invariably to a gas chamber.[23]

Despite the dark times, Viktor's life was flourishing in his position at the Rothschild Hospital. There he met Tilly Grosser, a nurse at the hospital, and they began dating. Viktor realized this romance was more important than his relationship to his parents. He had been toying with the idea of marrying Tilly, and then one day while she was preparing the noon meal with his parents, he received a call to perform emergency brain surgery. Returning several hours later, he assumed that his chance for lunch had passed. On his return, Tilly welcomed him with caring concern for the patient, and brought out his lunch that she had saved for him. These simple acts clinched Viktor's decision to ask Tilly to marry him, "Not because she was this or that. But because she was she."[24]

In December 1941, he made the first of two critical decisions of his life. After years of being unable to get an immigration visa, the American Consulate called Viktor to grant a visa. He hesitated because he knew that this would leave his parents in a vulnerable state. Viktor would later tell stories about how he prayed for a hint from heaven, and soon after that saw a piece of tile. Written upon it was a section from the Ten Commandments. It read, "Honor your father and your mother; that your days may be long in the land that God gives you." With that, Viktor had his answer and decided to let his visa lapse so he could protect his parents.[25]

Vienna had a separate marriage license office for Jews, and a public notice announced that the office would close on the last day of December 1941. With time limited, Viktor and Tilly took the plunge and were the second last couple to be married at this office. Coincidentally, the last couple was Viktor's high school history teacher from 20 years previous.[26]

After their marriage, Viktor and Tilly lived with Viktor's parents in their small flat. Within a few months, Tilly was pregnant. Unfortunately, the Nazis mandated that any Jewish woman who became pregnant would be sent to a concentration camp. The result was many Jewish women (including Tilly) having abortions. Later, Viktor dedicated his book *The Unheard Cry for Meaning* to this lost child.

Despite the forced abortion, this was the only time of relative calm in their marriage; Viktor felt that his position at the hospital would protect his family from deportation. However, the evil campaign toward Hitler's *Final Solution* was ramping up within Vienna. Eventually in late September 1942, the Frankls were called for deportation processing. Viktor reflected on these times: "But nobody who was not alive in that time can imagine the atmosphere, what it was like. You cannot imagine it!"[27]

The last Jews remaining in Vienna were apprehensive of the many deportations taking place. Viktor expected that any deportation would mean a forced resettlement in a Jewish ghetto in a large city outside Vienna. They expected inconvenience, and slum-like, confining, and uncomfortable conditions, but still tolerable until the end of the war. They hoped that their family, and Jewish friends, would all remain together, maintaining the community spirit during the deportation.

At first, the Frankls were all transported to *Theresienstadt*, a concentration camp and Jewish ghetto. The conditions surpassed Viktor's worst nightmares. It was there that Viktor last saw his parents, no longer able to protect them from their fates.

NOTES

1. Viktor E. Frankl, *Recollections: An Autobiography* (Cambridge, MA: Basic Books, 2000), 30–31.

2. A. S. Redsand, *Viktor Frankl: A Life Worth Living* (New York, NY: Clarion Books, 2006), 7.

3. Klingberg, *When Life Calls Out to Us* (New York, NY: Doubleday, 2001).

4. Viktor Frankl, *Recollections.* 27.

5. Ibid., 21–24.

6. Ibid., 46.

7. Ibid., 46–47.

8. Ibid., 48.

9. Ibid., 59.

10. Ibid., 50.

11. Ibid., 56.

12. Frankl, *Recollections*, 53.

13. Ibid., 60.

14. Ibid., 62–63.

15. Ibid., 64.

16. Ibid., 71.

17. Ibid., 67–68.

18. William Gould, *Frankl: Life with Meaning* (Pacific Grove, CA: Brooks/Cole Publishing, 1993), 5.

19. Ibid., 68.

20. A personal friend of Sigmund Freud wrote: "I decided to make a final effort to persuade Freud to change his mind. I had a heart to heart talk with Freud. As I had feared, he was bent on staying in Vienna." To my first plea, that he was not alone in the world and that his life was dear to many people, he replied with a sigh: "Alone, ah, if I were only alone I should long ago have done with life." A meeting of the Board of the Vienna Society had, however, been held on March 13 at which it was decided that everyone should flee the country if possible, and that the seat of the Society should be wherever Freud would settle . . . [after making arrangement] to me he wrote: "Two letters from you, to Anna and myself, arrived today. They are so refreshingly kind that I am moved to write to you at once without any external occasion but from an inner impulse. "I am sometimes perturbed by the idea that you might think we believe you are simply wishing to do your duty, without our appreciating the deep and sincere feelings expressed in your actions. I assure you this is not so, that we recognize your friendliness, count on it and fully reciprocate it. This is a solitary expression of my feelings, for between beloved friends much should be obvious and remain unexpressed." . . . [Freud's eldest children] reached London on May 16 and [Sigmund] on May 26."; Ernest Jones, *The life and work of Sigmund Freud* (New York: Basic Books, 1957), 219–226.

21. Ibid., 76.

22. Anna Redsand, *Viktor Frankl: A life worth living* (New York: Clarion Books, 2006), 50–59.

23 Ibid., 82.
24 Ibid., 86.
25 Ibid., 82–83.
26 Ibid., 87.
27. Klingberg, *When Life Calls Out to Us*, 33.

Chapter 2

The Camp Years

1942–1946

In 1942 Viktor Frankl, along with his wife and parents, were snared within the ever-widening Jewish deportation net. Even though Viktor had deliberately let his chance for a visa expire, he still thought that he had a safety net for his family with his job at the Rothschild Hospital. He was counting on that to protect them and keep them in Vienna. Unfortunately, the Nazis closed down the hospital and eventually selected the entire Frankl family for deportation.

In late September 1942, the Frankl family received the phone call telling them of their escorted pick-up the next morning. Viktor had to leave many prized possessions behind; among them were the postcards Freud had sent to him during his Gymnasium years. Also lost were some patient case histories written by Freud when he was in training at the University Psychiatric Clinic. Viktor received these from the keeper of the clinic archives.

On his last day in Vienna, Viktor approached the owner of the building, "A nice family – he was not Jewish and most of the residents in the building were Aryan. I told him that he could take from our flat whatever he wanted to keep it for himself or if we survived he could give it back to us if he wished."[1]

THERESIENSTADT

1942–1944

Viktor and Tilly, his parents Gabriel and Elsa, and Tilly's mother Emma, left together when the escorts showed up. They went to a collection point in Vienna and waited while others assembled with them. A day later, they left by train for an unknown destination. At Theresienstadt, a Nazi concentration camp and Jewish ghetto, the Frankls could not live together because there were separate living quarters for the young, the elderly, women, and men.

Not long after the Frankls arrived at Theresienstadt, an SS man selected Viktor for a trip to a local SS prison called the Small Fortress. Under the Nazi regime the Schutzstaffel, known as the SS, were the paramilitary Nazi fanatics responsible for enforcing Nazi racial policies. A friend of Viktor's had warned him to faint and fall to the ground should he be ordered to this location. Being too proud, Viktor failed to follow this advice. When he was ordered to this prison, he agreed, thinking he had little to fear. Upon arrival at the prison, Viktor discovered he was to provide the SS with the entertainment of performing senseless acts of work, running through the rain and throwing water on a compost heap. When he did not perform to their satisfaction, he was struck. Being hungry and tired, he was not able to satisfy their sadistic wishes and received a severe beating. As Viktor summarizes, "I was brought back to the ghetto with thirty-two injuries. Tilly saw me on the street in Theresienstadt and said, 'Viktor, for heaven's sake! What have they done to you!'"[2]

Viktor was assigned to live with six other physicians in two rooms of a barrack that included an infirmary and quarters for the elderly. Doctors were given special duties; Viktor's was to oversee a group of sick people. While the situation at Theresienstadt was deplorable, Viktor could at least still see his family every day. In addition, there were community activities, such as music, art, reading, lectures, and dramas.

At Theresienstadt, Viktor used his extensive experience with the suicidal to develop suicide intervention teams. The people on these teams would watch for signs of depression and despair in the barracks and then report potential suicide cases to Frankl for his intervention. His efforts were credited with a steep drop in suicides. Viktor's father, who was 81 when deported, became ill within 6 months of arrival at Theresienstadt. He died in February 1943 from starvation and pneumonia. Viktor had managed to smuggle a vial of morphine, which he used to ease his father's suffering during the last days. Viktor felt satisfied that he had done what he could do; he had stayed in Vienna to help his elderly parents, and he spared his father unnecessary suffering at the end of his life.

After spending 2 years at Theresienstadt, in October 1944, Viktor's name appeared on the list of transports, those being moved to other camps. All he knew was that he was on Transport East. When Tilly heard of Viktor's transport, she volunteered to go with him, even though she had a job in a munitions factory and was safe from transports. Viktor begged her not to volunteer because they did not know the transport's destination; it could be someplace worse than Theresienstadt.[3]

When Viktor and Tilly left, only Viktor's mother remained of the original family group that arrived in Theresienstadt. She was 65, and Viktor hoped that she would survive by avoiding transport and remaining at Theresienstadt.

AUSCHWITZ AND THE PHASE OF SHOCK

1944

During the rail transport, Viktor discovered they were heading to Poland, and this likely meant Auschwitz. Viktor knew something of Auschwitz's reputation by this time. Auschwitz was the largest Nazi extermination camp. Specifically, it was a system of camps in Poland, consisting of three main ones – Auschwitz I, II, and III – and many sub-camps in the surrounding area. There were already 100,000 prisoners there when Viktor and Tilly arrived. They arrived at an Auschwitz camp called Birkenau, and the conditions were far harsher than those at Theresienstadt. The overcrowded camp with lacking enough water and sanitation, resulting in the rapid spread of disease.

These harsh circumstances forced Viktor to look for meaning in such conditions; paradoxically they may have helped him to advance his fledgling theories of psychotherapy. Where he had given up the chance to go to the United States to advance his studies, now life itself forced him to live with the problem that he had struggled with in theory. Viktor was tasting defeat and discovering meaning in the reality of irrevocable commitments and acts. What he had previously struggled to clarify in theory, in the boundaries of self and outlook, experience now made porous and permeable. Viktor became alive to the puzzle of living in these conditions, and found truth in seeming contradictions, striving to unify opposites in mind and experience. For Viktor, the challenge was not in facing the great horrors of living in the concentration camps. Rather, the test was in drawing meanings from the mass of smaller torments that faced daily existence.

Often prisoners took on functionary tasks, as assigned by the SS running of the camps. The SS supervised these functionaries, or *Capos*, who ran the camp. As Viktor paints the picture of the common prisoner in his memoirs, he demonstrates that it was not simply the Nazi captors that contributed to the hellish conditions he endured. It was the common prisoners whom the Capos truly hated. The Capos often fared better in camp than in their lives during peacetime, living in relative luxury while the common prisoner starved. Inwardly Viktor bristled at the cruelty of the Capos, and he believed this inclination for cruelty is why the SS selected them.[4]

In Auschwitz, Viktor saw the ever-present tensions and contradictions of life, and just how fragile life was, as it became a relentless fight for life. He watched civilized fellow prisoners devolve into intense fighting over transport selection. All that seemed to matter was that one's own name was crossed off the list of victims.

The experience was not one of pure philosophical insights for Viktor, that came later, and during brief moments when he felt strong enough. In general, Viktor struggled to stay alive in a context where human contact was lacking humanity. People had neither time nor desire to consider moral or ethical issues. Every person seemed to be driven by the instinct to survive at all costs. Yet, on the rare occasion, Viktor took solace in small achievements. He found that these moments revealed experiences of meaning, and reinforced his inherent ideas about the importance of meaning.

As Number 119,104, he had lost much of his identity, but he was still able to experience little meanings by working extra hard at his job of digging a tunnel for a railway line. The special jobs he took on received a payment of six cigarettes, which he was then able to exchange with other prisoners for twelve soups.[5] Sadly, he noted that people who chose to keep the cigarettes had lost the will to live and wanted to enjoy their last days. Viktor realized once a prisoner lost the will to live, it rarely returned.

Viktor sought to help these people by trying to clarify how to experience meaning in life, even in Auschwitz. It was a time when he began to realize just how important meaning can be for human survival, in this case his. This led him to try to clarify the sufferings he witnessed, and sometimes experienced. On reflection, Viktor recognized a predictable sequence of stages that a prisoner went through in adjusting to the extremities of camp life. He identified three phases of the inmate's mental reactions to camp life: (1) the shock of admission, (2) the period of being immersed in camp routine, and (3) the period following release and liberation.

The prisoner's first phase was a completely shocking one.[6] Viktor wasn't immune to its presence, as this phase was visceral and overwhelming. The terror of the public presence of death that pervaded his first few hours of internment left him numb. Horrifying as the first moments were, the numbing shock prepared him for the discovery of even greater evils. Later, in his clinical analysis of this shock, he came to understand something of the self-deception strategies that people use in dealing with these images of death. The self-deceiving trick of the mind known as the *delusion of reprieve*. The doomed person, immediately before death, gets the illusion of reprieve as the mind grasps desperately for hope in the face of death.

One aspect of this first phase came from realizing how a simple flick of an officer's wrist or finger could determine one's fate. One time Viktor was in a selection line. As Viktor approached the SS officer, he stood up as tall and firm as possible, the SS man stopped him. Placed his shoulders squarely on Viktor's shoulders and then turned him slightly to the right, and Viktor moved to that side. The SS officer then went back to directing people casually, to the right or to the left. The officer with his right hand lifted, and forefinger pointing leisurely, decided in a moment who lived and who died.[7]

Later Viktor discovered the meaning of that selection process. During the first selection at the Auschwitz camp system, the majority were sent to a building that had the word "bath" written over its doors in several European languages. Each prisoner received a bar of soap, and sent in large groups into the building; where they were killed by gassing.

After this first selection, Viktor asked other prisoners how he could find his friend. They simply asked which direction he was sent during the selection. Viktor said his friend was sent to the left. The prisoner replied with a long look and head nod toward the large chimneys in the distance. "That's where your friend is, floating up to Heaven,"[8] was the answer. But Viktor still did not understand until he learned the truth in plain words that the chimneys were crematoriums and his friend was dead.

The early shock became even deeper when anything that once made Viktor feel special outside of camp was taken away. Personally meaningful achievements meant nothing. This, coupled with the bitter uncaring attitude of experienced prisoners, left Viktor feeling like the camp stole his humanity. On that first day, Viktor tried to take an old prisoner into his confidence. Viktor lifted his coat, showing the old prisoner his book manuscript sewn into the inner pocket of his coat. Viktor tried to explain that he was hiding a great scientific work that he must keep at all costs. Slowly the old prisoner grinned, first piteous, then more amused, mocking, and insulting, until he spat out one word: "Shit!"[9] For Viktor, this word marked his full immersion into the first phase of psychological adjustment to camp life; for with that word his former life was gone.

Loss of significance and control, as well as emotional isolation, negatively impacted Viktor. In addition, there was the loss of his intellectual child, the book sewn into his coat. Then finally all vestiges of human dignity disappeared, as each prisoner stood outside, cold and naked. All Viktor now possessed, was his naked existence. All material vestiges of his former life were gone.

PHASE TWO: ADJUSTING TO CAMP LIFE AND LESSONS OF SURVIVAL

1944–1945

Viktor watched as prisoners' illusions of hope disappeared, one by one. Then, unexpectedly, a grim sense of humor struck the prisoners. They knew that they had nothing to lose except their own outlandishly naked lives. At that moment, in the midst of the loss of all hope or identity, what was left was something unexpected, fun. So, for a few brief moments, Viktor, along with the other prisoners standing there naked, tried to make fun of each other.

Apart from the humor, a new way of looking at the world began to settle over the prisoners as they adjusted into what Viktor identified as the second phase of psychological adjustment, learning about camp life. An early feature of this second phase was sheer cold curiosity in learning how to fit into this new reality. It meant giving up old beliefs and learning new truths. This emotionless attitude hung over Auschwitz, as prisoners became detached from the surroundings and other people. Viktor watched as people developed a grim sense of anticipation of what will happen next. Viktor also took on this grim attitude of new experiences and their surprising effects. He was especially surprised when he was stuck outside on a cold day, naked, in the rain, and did not get sick. Viktor found his health remained through the harshest of circumstances and starvation.

Viktor discovered that while adjustment to camp life was difficult, it was possible. A truth settled over Viktor's mind, a realization that people can get used to anything, no matter how horrible, degrading, or stressful it is; in the face of all reason, people can get used to anything.

Despite adapting, Viktor was soon entertaining suicide as a real alternative to camp life. He realized the danger of such thoughts, and made a promise never to run into the electrified barbed wire fence. He knew how easy it was to fall victim to this temptation, for he watched it become a popular method of suicide in Auschwitz. In spite of this personal pact, at times he was so overwhelmed, even the threat of death in the gas chambers held little sway over him. After all, death by gas chamber would save him the trouble of having to commit suicide.

Viktor soon found that while settling into camp life, he must still be mindful of his existence. Beyond having a positive mental attitude, it also meant that Viktor must work hard on his outward appearance. He soon received a reminder of just how essential this was for his survival. Smuggling himself into their block, a man came to share some news and advice. This man told everyone to use whatever glass they could find to shave each morning, taking special care to scrap their cheeks to look young and ruddy. The man then affirmed that if they all walked smartly, stood tall, and shaved regularly, they did not need fear being selected for the gas chambers. The man then looked at Viktor, advising him to take special care, to avoid being gassed the next day.

After a few weeks, Viktor was firmly in the grasp of the second phase; the phase of relative apathy in which he achieved an emotional death. Whereas prisoners during the first phase felt shock at the brutality, in the second phase they became numb and apathetic to sufferings. The sufferers, the dying, and the dead became such commonplace sights that prisoners simply felt nothing.

Viktor too fell into an apathetic emotional death; there was no longer room for shock. His feelings were dark and the most horrific of scenes did not trigger his internal emotional alarms. At times, he could simply sit and eat his soup, as people walked in front of him, dragging fresh dead bodies along the floor.

THE POWER OF IMAGINATION

Apathy, thought Viktor, was a necessary mechanism of self-defense. Though he was apathetic, there were still moments of joy, as he daydreamed and played in his own imagination. With this, Viktor helped clarify the power of imagination in survival, visualizing a wished future event to be already present.

This visualization strategy was powerful for Viktor, as he focused on what he hoped for. By actively engaging that positive image in the present, Viktor pushed the apathy out of his experience, bringing a moment of internal peace and joy. It allowed him to operate, if only for short moments, in a life-affirming state of mind. The most powerful themes for Viktor were relationships to hold, a love, and a commitment: key themes that were to later become integral in Logotherapy. Viktor himself would allow his mind to cling to images of his wife in glorious detail. He would hear her voice, smell her scent, see her smile, and almost feel her touch. The mere thought carried his emotions to a positive idealized place. A poetic wisp of love filled his soul, pulling his attention away from the horrible, desolate condition of his objective reality. At times, a guard's voice or whip would yank him back to reality, but he would quickly return to the image of his wife, asking her questions. Losing himself in a make-believe conversation of love.

While Viktor could daydream some peaceful times with his wife, his objective existence lay in sharp contrast. Life with the Auschwitz work gangs, especially during the winter months, was full of shouts and insults that tore as deeply as the cold. It was partly this contrast between the external world of bitter anger and Viktor's inner world of love that helped him clarify the importance of love within Logotherapy. Through this experience, he became aware that love is a critical means for experiencing meaning.

As the prisoners worked with their spade or pickax, the supervisors shouted insults at them. The ground was often hard, frozen, and unforgiving. The conditions were dark and dirty. Yet Viktor set his heart on love. He discovered that love for someone goes far beyond the beloved and into the deepest of human meanings, to the heart of a person's spiritual being and the inner self. At that point, objective realities lost their importance, for nothing could touch the strength of that love.

As the inner life of Viktor's mind become more intense, he also experienced the beauty of art and nature as never before. At times, in the camp, people would draw the attention of a prisoner next to him, to a beautiful view of the tall Bavarian trees. Often puddles of water and mud surrounded the desolate gray mud huts the prisoners lived within. Yet, Viktor could create a spiritual experience by gazing into the water and seeing the reflected sky blue beauty. Such experiences were little reminders that even in a place of damp darkness and death, a whisper of hope and beauty survived. Transcending all the hopelessness to shine into a Viktor's soul.

These experiences offered Viktor the realization that one can frame reality with an imagination of hope. It was a maxim that he would take with him throughout his professional career. He was more resilient when infused with hope, through the power of his imagination. For Viktor, his stance toward his situation was important, and he found strength to take this stand through his imagination.

THE POWER OF HUMOR

Viktor was as a funny man. Humor then became a powerful tool for his self-preservation. Humor, for Viktor, was a special human quality that lets people rise above any situation. Humor was a divine quality that allows people to create perspective, to put distance between the self and any danger.

As time wore on, Viktor received transfer orders out of his Auschwitz camp to Kaufering, in the Dachau camp network. This was a strangely joyful surprise that put all the new arrivals in a good mood, including Viktor. The wish of his hut warden in Auschwitz had come true. This new camp did not have a chimney – unlike Auschwitz. This meant no gas chambers and no mass killing of prisoners. On realizing this, Viktor and his camp-mates laughed and cracked jokes, despite standing outside on a cold rainy night, while officials searched for a missing prisoner. Despite the punishment parade, Viktor and the other prisoners were very pleased!

THE POWER OF DUTY

Viktor discovered that often, taking up one's duty and responsibility was more powerful than the psychological apathy that constantly threatened the prisoner. A realization took hold in Viktor's mind that being responsible to something, whether a person or conscience, was essential to overcome apathy. Within Viktor's own experience, after a few days in the sick quarters at Kaufering, a camp affiliated with Dachau, the chief doctor asked Viktor to volunteer for medical duties in another camp containing typhus patients. His sense of duty as a doctor outweighed the urgent advice of his friends. He volunteered knowing that it may mean his own death. Viktor thought that if he were to die, at least he had taken an opportunity to add meaning to his life.

Viktor soon transferred from Kaufering to Turkheim, the camp for sick prisoners, but it was still not an easy existence. Though busy, Viktor found a place of relative solitude behind an earthen hut where he worked with over fifty delirious prisoners. He would sit on his heels upon a raised wooden shaft whenever he was not working. Viktor would just sit and star out of the camp, out at the green slopes and the beauty of the distant hills.

The power of doing one's duty clearly became an important part of his psychological repertoire. It seemed that even in the face of the horrid circumstances of a prison camp full of death, doing his duty as a doctor gave him the strength to continue to survive. This, coupled with the recognition that he had the power to choose how he engaged the experience, rounded out his sense of personal empowerment.

THE POWER OF CHOICE

Another lesson that Viktor learned during his camp years was the power of choice or, more accurately, the sense of helplessness that came from a fear of decision making. Sometimes this meant choosing to stay at Kaufering to help his patients, even when an opportunity to escape presented itself.

Viktor made this tormenting choice, as the battlefront drew nearer, and he had an opportunity to escape with a friend. Under the pretense of holding a consultation about a patient whose illness needed a specialist's advice, a fellow inmate was to smuggle Viktor out. Outside the camp, a member of the foreign resistance movement was to supply them with uniforms and documents. Although Viktor did not share his intent, a patient guessed. In a weak sickly voice he asked Viktor directly if he was escaping, but Viktor denied it. Viktor's conscience soon got the best of him, knowing that he could not, in good conscience, leave his patients. He went out and told his cohort that he was going to stay. At that moment, the anxiety and depressive feeling that had hung over Viktor for a time, left him. This choice, he discovered, had renewed him in some way, and he could face whatever came next.

Before this time, Viktor had found it hard to make choices, owing this partly to a sense of inferiority because of camp life. His loss of identity meant losing part of his power to choose. Logically then, choosing something within camp life was something that Viktor found to be a supremely self-defining act. This was a general truth for all inmates; prior to camp life all inmates were *somebody*. Now treated like worthless trash, they lost the basic confidence needed. It took the step of anchoring one's inner value in higher, more spiritual unshakable things, to be able to make positive choices in one's camp life. For Viktor, he found this in his faith, and his identity as a doctor.

In the end, Viktor's decision not to escape was moot. As he and his friend decided, for the second time to escape, that day the doors to the camp opened. Representatives of the International Red Cross arrived from Geneva, declaring protection of inmates.

Despite the hope of freedom, that night the SS arrived with trucks to transfer the prisoners, claiming orders to move them to Switzerland in an exchange of prisoners of war. A lack of space meant Viktor was not allowed on the trucks, and was bitterly disappointed that evening. Little did he know how fortunate he was to have missed the final transport. For that night the fighting reached the camp, and surrendered to the Americans the next morning. Weeks later, Viktor discovered that those taken in the trucks were burned alive by the Nazi SS guards.

Through these final camp experiences, Viktor believed that choice of action is essential to human existence. Camp life affirmed to Viktor that people do have a choice of action. He became convinced that people can preserve a vestige of independence and spiritual freedom, even in the most terrible of conditions.

This realization of the power of choice in all circumstances led to one of Viktor's deepest insights for living a meaningful life. The realization that *we experience meaning through electing an attitude taken toward circumstances.* For the way in which we accept an unchangeable fate and all the suffering it entails gives us opportunity, even under the most difficult circumstances, to add a deeper meaning to life.

Ultimately, Viktor's lessons about the power of choice became central to his logotherapeutic approach. The many lessons learned within the Nazi camps helped refine his theoretical perspective on human existence. These lessons also confirmed that imagination, humor, a sense of duty, and personal choice are essential to continued existence in the face of challenges.

ATTITUDE

Attitude, Viktor discovered, is central to the experience of meaning. A spiritual attitude can drive away despair toward one's eventual mortality. The chosen attitude that Viktor believes important is not a defeatist attitude. He believed that people should muster the courage to choose, despite the provisional existence of life. The light that concentration camp life shines on this problem is that it was a provisional existence of unknown limit. It is an attitude of embracing life, fully recognizing the absence of security in life.

This lack of security also made it clear to Viktor just how important future goals are, however provisional they may be. He saw just how important it was for people to choose toward a certain future, at the same time recognizing the tenuous nature of that future. It is recognized that individuals have a responsibility to choose attitude and action, authentically engaging life. To abdicate that responsibility was to deny any place for future goals, the result being a drawing inward, depression, and giving up on life.

For Viktor, it was not a mere looking ahead with blind hope. It was an active, personal meaning discovered and simultaneously chosen; it was a meaning owned that made the difference. Meaning, for Viktor, had actual survival value and was the source of strength in all circumstances. A great deal of inner strength could be drawn from a future goal chosen. Viktor would often reflect upon Nietzsche's maxim that a person who has a *why* to live for can bear with almost any *how*.

MEANING AND RESPONSIBILITY

Viktor saw that the concentration camps revealed the position of meaning in life. Meaning was a source of unbelievable levels of resilience. This revelation was no more true than during the days and weeks following camp liberation. As Viktor's emancipation finally came, like a beautiful dream, so also came the flood of nightmarish memories. In the midst of it all, Viktor realized that he now had nothing left to fear from life and could truly live in fear of God alone.

The realization that meaning is powerful when lived and brings out another key theme within Viktor's Logotherapy: the personal and dynamic aspect of meaning. Meaning is not an intellectual or abstract value for Viktor. Meaning is discovered, experienced, and lived out in choices that engage the circumstances of life. Life is therefore not an inert, dispassionate object that we relate with.

The content of meaning in life may differ from person to person, and even from day to day. What matters therefore is not the general meaning of life, but rather the personal, chosen, and enacted meanings within a person's life in the given moment. Meaning is a moment-to-moment experience. So, Viktor began to see that asking about the general meaning of life was fundamentally the wrong question. Rather, Viktor envisioned life asking the question to each person, as to the meaning of each individual life in the moment. The task of a person then is to respond to life's question, answering life from moment to moment through actions of responsibility.

Responsibility in action and choices then comes to summarize Viktor's understanding of living out meaning, of essentially writing the meaning of one's life. Active *responsibleness* is the categorical imperative of Logotherapy, where every choice is toward a responsible goal.[10]

Viktor also believed in a spirituality of humanness. This firmly plants his Logotherapy as an existential, yet spiritually informed approach, with a role for love,[11] suffering, and trusting in a deeper – meaning within life.

> This ultimate meaning necessarily exceeds and surpasses the futile intellectual capacities of man; in Logotherapy, we speak in this context of a super-meaning. What is demanded of man is not, as some existential philosophers teach, to endure the meaninglessness of life, but rather to bear his incapacity to grasp its unconditional meaningfulness in rational terms. *Logos* is deeper than logic.[12]

SUMMARY

In summary, while Viktor claims to have developed his ideas before the camp years, his experiences forced him to clarify and solidify them. His ideas became deeper and more personal, recognizing the contingency of life. He personally experienced the temptation of suicide and the need to face death to reclaim his humanity. Viktor discovered life's potential for meaning, even in conditions of extreme suffering and death. The mere reality of experience, Viktor realized, moves it from contingency to fact. Death or suffering can never steal personal experiences; they are safe in the realm of meaningful experiences forever.

For Viktor, the past is a secure storehouse where nothing is lost; life is irrevocably gathered. Thus, the vapor of our existence in no way makes it meaningless. Rather our capacity to experience meaningful living through responsibility, in serving and loving others, hinges on this. Our good choices rest on realizing the essential transitory possibilities and acting on them. For in making responsible choices, we move existence from the contingency, and pull it into the fullness of reality. Viktor was never tired of pointing out that people usually bemoan the temporary nature of life and forget that the past stores all. When life's experiences move from the present moment to the past, they are locked and forever secure. Past experiences exist in the surest form of being.

For Viktor, people are self-defining beings. They have great freedom to take a stand toward the conditions that surround them. Even the concentration camp prisoners could choose an attitude and a meaning to live. At the same time, people are finite beings, and freedom is restricted. It is not independence from conditions, but it is the liberty to take a stand against the conditions.

A human being is supremely self-determining according to Viktor. A person becomes an existential being, within limits of genes, aptitude, and environment, through choices. For Viktor, his experience within the camps was a living laboratory that proved that circumstances alone do not determine behavior.

Life is meaningful in all circumstances. To experience this breadth of meaning often relies on the human ability to turn negatives into positives. For Viktor, when a person lives out responsibility and makes strong choices, these actions can reveal blessings in any situation. Meaning, for Viktor, was the treasure to strive for in times of suffering. Viktor often compared meaning to laughter; for if you want a person to laugh, you must give the person a reason. So too, when meaning is experienced, it improves life, bringing happiness and a means to cope with suffering.

Herein is the essential value of Viktor's Logotherapy, as it was tested and refined through his camp experiences. Logotherapy teaches that there are three pathways through which one arrives at meaning. The first path is creating a work or by doing a deed. The second path is by experiencing some work, or some love of person, task, or experience. The third and most important path is choosing an attitude. Meaning is experienced by turning a personal heartbreak into a joy. In the end, the greatest lesson Viktor learned during his concentration camp years was, where there is meaning, despair disappears.

NOTES

1. Klingberg, *When Life Calls Out to Us*, 109.
2. Ibid., 113.
3. Ibid.
4. Frankl, *Man's Search for Meaning,* 22.
5. Ibid., 25.
6. Ibid.
7. Ibid., 30.
8. Ibid., 31.
9. Ibid., 33.
10. Ibid.
11. According to Frankl, love was the best way to relate with and honor another human being. A person, for Frankl, cannot be truly encountered except through an attitude of love. This encounter should be aware of what a person can be.
12. Frankl, *Man's Search for Meaning,* 141.

Chapter 3

Postwar Years

1945–1947

THE THIRD PHASE

The day the white flag rose above the camp gates, freeing Viktor from Nazi hands, he entered the third psychological phase of concentration camp prisoners: bitterness and loss. It did not happen right away; he was far too weak those first days. He spent all his effort going past the gates and rediscovering the freedom to walk through the meadow. That first evening he could not feel any joy over the liberation, he had no strength.

While others wanted to kill the administrator of the camp, Viktor knew him to be a fair and kind man. After all, Turkheim was a camp for sick prisoners, not a death camp like Auschwitz. A few prisoners hid the administrator in the woods and negotiated with the Americans to have him surrender only after assurances of his safety were secured. This was the start of Viktor's recovery through the third phase, for he was choosing the path of responsibility, in spite of his growing realization of all he had lost.

In the months following his liberation from the camp, Viktor was too weak to travel. Instead, he found work at the hospital near Turkheim. Not knowing the fate of his mother or his wife Tilly, Viktor finally headed back to Vienna, once the border opened between Germany and Austria. In August 1945, four months after his liberation from the camps, Viktor arrived back in Vienna. The majestic public buildings were ruins, and the thriving Jewish community was all but gone. It was during the first few days back in Vienna that Viktor heard rumors of the deaths of Tilly, his mother, his brother, and his sister-in-law. Although he was in the city where he spent his entire life, Viktor developed an odd feeling for it. Viktor suffered from the moral deformity that was to be expected from his death camp experiences. Then came the bitterness and disillusionment as he tried to return to his former life. His inner struggle, he was sure, was shared by others who were also met with, "A shrug of the shoulders and with hackneyed phrases."[1]

He took solace in the knowledge that after experiencing the horrors of camp life, he had nothing left to fear, except God. In looking back, he realized the importance of choosing responsibility within life, and this confirmed his ideas about psychotherapy. Viktor had the opportunity to escape the harsh realities of Nazi-occupied Austria. He could have escaped to chase his dream of writing and promoting his ideas of psychotherapy. Yet his sense of personal duty to his parents meant that he chose to stay in Vienna; this allowed him to care for his parents.

This choice to follow the path of responsibility led him through the Nazi death camps. Viktor was now a man with nothing. He had lost his parents and spouse, and the records of his scientific work. Now with the end of the war, he was slowly rebuilding his life, and this meant fulfilling his dream of writing the book he lost. This marked the birth of Logotherapy was born, as its key tenets were finally written down in Viktor's first book.

THE DOCTOR AND THE SOUL

The first book Viktor published immediately after returning to Vienna, *The Doctor and the Soul*, conceptually predated his time in the Nazi concentration camps. The media often portrays his time within the worst of human suffering to be the impetus for this radical new therapy. The fact is such experiences simply confirmed and refined his ideas. He hid a manuscript in his shirt upon his arrest, but lost it: "Under those circumstances I felt like a father who was not spared watching his children murdered before his eyes. The book was, in fact, my spiritual child who I'd hoped would survive even if I did not do so myself."[2]

Within camp life, Viktor was able to deepen, confirm, and elaborate his ideas. The key was his ability to test the importance of meaning, observing others and himself undergoing the horrific treatment at Auschwitz and other concentration camps. His model was clearly sound, for the *will to meaning*, Viktor found, has actual survival value. Viktor personally used it to survive his own hellish experiences. "I succeeded somehow in rising above the situation, above the sufferings of the moment, and I observed them as if they were already of the past."[3]

After the war Viktor decided to again put his words to print. During his first weeks back in Vienna, he looked up Paul Polak; it was there that Viktor collapsed in despair over his many losses and the pain of living alone. Viktor burst into tears, crying to his friend, "Paul, I must tell you, that when all this happens to someone, to be tested in such a way, that it must have some meaning. I have a feeling – and I don't know how else to say it – that something waits for me. That something is expected of me, that I am destined for something."[4]

A short time later, the new chief of psychiatry at the University of Vienna, urged Viktor to write the final draft of *The Doctor and the Soul.* Viktor was full of emptiness and loneliness. Realizing he needed a task that was meaningful and worthwhile, he buried himself in the work of completing the manuscript. His emotions, still fresh and raw, transformed the book from the dispassionate academic work it may have been before war. Now the words flowed from his existence, both as a psychiatrist and as a long-suffering man. Working in a sparsely equipped room, the windows were broken and covered with cardboard, affording little natural light. Viktor paced around, dictating his thoughts to stenographer-typists working in shifts, tears flowing down his face. His mind moved by overwhelming emotions and painful memories.[5]

THE NEED FOR LOGOTHERAPY

In *The Doctor and the Soul*, Viktor finally outlines the basic theory and practice of Logotherapy (literally, healing through meaning). In doing psychotherapy, Viktor wants others to recognize that a person is not simply biology, nor simply a jumble of symptoms. The patient has a mental lived world and a spirituality. Viktor's wish was for psychiatrists to recognize the essential humanness of their patients. The *will to meaning* is a powerful human force that is essential for emotional healing and resiliency.

The essence of Logotherapy was identifying and encouraging the *will to meaning* of the patient. Logotherapy places the spiritual and meaning dimensions back in the doctor-patient relationship. For Frankl, a doctor who ignores the *will to meaning* is complicit in perpetuating a patient's suffering of the *existential frustration* or *noogenic neurosis.*

Logotherapy is not to replace existing psychotherapy, rather to complement it, by reminding therapists that patients have a human longing for meaning. When therapy directs attention to the full human spirit, it is better able to deal with the very human spiritual distress that often occurs in people's lives. Sexual frustration can lead to a neurosis, so too, a spiritual frustration or frustration of the will to meaning may also lead to a neurosis. Logotherapy is therefore a psychotherapeutic adjunct, that help clients to cope with their existential frustration.[6]

Frankl admits there is a time and a place for Logotherapy, just as there is for pharmacological treatment. Yet even in the face of certain suffering and death, where the doctor can do nothing more medically, he can still engage in a type of meaning therapy that Frankl calls *medical ministry.* This medical ministry essentially helps the patient find the courage to face this suffering with grace and dignity. The crux of Logotherapy is simply to help people discover meaning within life. This comes about, according to Frankl, in three forms: First is creative values, like achieving a task or doing something. Second is experiential values, like experiencing the beauty in something or someone. Third is attitudinal values, like choosing one's orientation to the way that the world deals with you. As Frankl points out, "Logotherapy is ultimately education toward responsibility; the patient must push forward independently toward the concrete meaning of his own existence."[7]

Logotherapy is an aide to general psychotherapy, ensuring the dimension of meaning remains. Just as psychoanalysis brings the unconscious to consciousness for healing, so too does Logotherapy. Yet the analytic techniques focusing on dynamics alone is too limited and one sided. As such, Logotherapy provides the counterweight balance to Freudian psychoanalytic practice. According to Frankl, "Each is right about the side of reality that it sees; but only both sides together can produce a rounded picture of the psychic life."[8]

THE STRUGGLE WITH RELIGIOUS MEANING

It took nine years before Frankl's first book was translated into English. After the war, an American commission scouted Europe for books that would be suitable for English translation. Frankl's book was the only Austrian work selected. The American edition's title, *The Doctor and the Soul*, was disliked by Frankl. He felt English terms such as *soul* and *spirit* carried strong religious connotations, and he would have preferred a title less connected with religion. He wanted to appeal to a wide audience of readers, and he did not want to deter readers with a title suggesting a book with religious content. Despite this, it is a deeply spiritual book dealing with spirituality as the deep core, conscience of human experience.

Frankl points out that all people are spiritual. As such, the religious connotations of the term *spiritual* should not be given too much emphasis. All psychotherapy at its core helps bring what is unconscious into conscious awareness; Logotherapy is no different. It promotes personal awareness of individual responsibility – the essential ground for human existence.

Responsibility is central to Logotherapy, as it implies a sense of obligation. A person's obligation is a *meaning* – the specific meaning of a person's life. Meaning questions are of supreme interest to the patient, and come up especially with a patient racked by spiritual conflict. The therapist doesn't need to bring up the subject; the patient in spiritual distress flings the question out. Whether clear or implicit, this is an intrinsically human question, "What is the point of my life?" Meaning of life struggles shouldn't be taken as mental illness itself; it is the truest expression of being human.

Sadly, questions of meaning are often cast aside by the therapist as morbid states that are symptoms of a mental illness. Logotherapy clarifies for the doctor or therapist that the search for meaning is essential and healthy. People are beings that need to make meaning, have meaning, and live meaning. Logotherapy also points out that a human life is set by a historical context, framing the meaning-making process.

Frankl points out that the person of religion already has the means to live and create meaning in life, and find the meaning of life. People need to simply limit the scope of their search. Learning to explore the question personally and practically, like "What is the meaning of my choice in this moment?" In addition, the religious person has access to a *super-meaning*, a place to locate personal meaning. Both are essential to gain a full experience of meaning. The challenge is finding the balance. We shouldn't begin with grand questions like, the meaning of life in general, for that is beyond our grasp.

As Frankl notes about the Book of Job, when God asked Job to explain how God made the earth and the universe, Job simply replied by covering his mouth. Job knew there was no way he could know the answer. By this illustration, Frankl demonstrates that we need a *super-meaning* or overarching narrative of the universe. Our minds need this guiding story to form our worldview. Its details still impenetrable to our finite minds. Frankl quotes Schleich, "God sat at the organ of possibilities and improvised the world. Poor creatures that we are, we men can only hear the vox humana (the human voice) . . . that is so beautiful, how glorious the Whole must be."[9] A genuine faith then provides a *super-meaning*, according to Frankl, that is, an anchor to inner strength, and adds immeasurably to human vitality. To such faith there is nothing meaningless, nothing in vain.[10]

VALUES IN LOGOTHERAPY

The Doctor and the Soul outlines foundational ideas of Logotherapy. A principle philosophy behind Logotherapy is that humanity is about being conscious and responsible. Responsibility emerges in the actualizing of values, both eternal and situation-specific values. Opportunities change from person to person and from situation to situation. However, the drive of being fully human still involves values actualization. This is what living a human life is about, and where meaning is experienced. It is at the heart of being human to express values through improving the lives of others.

The meaning of being a person then comes into fulfillment through engaging the world and being in community, for the value of the individual is somewhat dependent upon the community. Similarly, if the community is to have meaning, it must hold the individuality of people within it. Hegemony, however, submerges the single unique existence, for uniqueness disrupts the control of any mass. Community then constitutes relationships of individuality. Hegemonic mass erases individuality, while in the community it emerges.

Frankl even goes beyond this to point out that human uniqueness and singularity are vital to the meaning of existence. This singularity defies quantification, for quantification removes the value to the whole. A fingerprint may be unique and quantifiable. However, a fingerprint does not establish the fullness of the humanness of the person. Frankl then draws on the analogy of Hegel's *good* and *bad* infinity – to speak of a good and a bad uniqueness. *Good uniqueness* is the fullness of a person's individuality directed toward others and community. In this good uniqueness there is real unquantifiable value.[11]

Unlike some other schools of existentially informed therapy, Logotherapy does not subscribe to pure constructivism. Frankl views *meaning* as a discovery process, something with a context, engagement, and discovery. Meaning is already woven into the very fabric of existence. There are many small potential discoveries, with no grand singular meaning to life (at least not one that can be easily grasped). Frankl prefers to view this discovery of meaning as not a question that we ask and expect to receive an intellectual answer. Rather, life asks the question, and we are to respond by choosing actions in living life, and only after engaging does the meaning reveal itself. We discover meaning through experiencing meaning. Only at the end of life can we discern some larger meaning of an individual life.

A person's experience of meaning, for Frankl, comes best when the person listens to the conscience. The conscience is the inner voice that speaks to the person. It guides you on how to respond to life's question of how you will live. Conscience is always a response to a situation. For Frankl, this voice of conscience is another reason why the religious person is better able to find meaning in existence. For, in this most personal of experiences, it isn't simply an inner voice of self; it is the still small voice of God speaking to the person's experience.

Every moment for a person is a dialogue with life, a challenge to meet the concrete demands called for by life. To discover and express values through personal engagement. One way meaning reveals itself is when people passively receive the world. This may be the experience of nature, or of some art form or other life event. Meaning also emerges from choosing an attitude, which echoes the saying, "You cannot direct the wind, but you can adjust your sails." From the manner in which a person takes these things upon the self comes a multitude of values and meanings.[12]

Creating something is another way people reveal meaning that is hidden in the world, the sheer act of immersing into an action or work. Engagement in work or creativity to reveal meaning is a rather easy notion for most people to apprehend. Most people strive for success, to do something great to experience a meaning. Creative value does not reside in the greatness of the work. Recognition of a great work is therefore separate from the meaning experienced in creating a work. Indeed very often the most meaningful moments are those that are experienced by only one or two other people apart from the self; or maybe only by the self. Therefore, baking a loaf of bread for a dear friend and providing a meaningful, caring, enjoyable meal can be as full of meaning as writing an award winning novel. It is not then the size of the creative venture that gives it value (great works or small ones) but the fact that it was expressed at all in the act of it being created.

Meaning discovery is often a counterintuitive process. For example, those who are driven to seeking happiness and financial success rarely find deep meaning. When people pause and consider their everyday experience and existence, they see that they ascribe value and meaning to in small moments. Meaningful moments have nothing to do with wealth or success, and are clearly independent of both. The therapist's role in Logotherapy is to educate the patient. Resiliency of the patient may then increase by engagement in small, meaningful experiences.

So, values within Logotherapy are a structural means for the therapist to help the patient discover and experience meaning in life. Meaning can be experienced, according to Logotherapy, through the realization of creative action. In addition, there is meaning that can be realized in experience. A third avenue to discovering meaning lies precisely in the client's attitude toward the limiting factors upon his life.

It is important to note that Frankl does not consider Logotherapy to be a rational therapy that is completely detached from the client's life. Rather, Logotherapy is a vital call to the patient to translate values into concrete duties, cast in the form of the demands of each day and in personal tasks. The experience of the meaning comes through the engagement in these tasks. As Frankl makes clear, "The conviction that one has a task before him has enormous psychotherapeutic and psychogenic value. We venture to say that nothing is more likely to help a person."[13]

LIVING IN A FRUITFUL TENSION

For Frankl, meaning in life, even in the presence of suffering, is discovered not in philosophizing, but in actualizing creative values, experiential values, and attitudinal values. Here then we discover the meaning of suffering, or rather the meaning to be found within the experience of suffering. In suffering from something we move inward away from it, we establish a distance between our personality and this something. As long as we are still suffering from a condition that ought not to be, we remain in a state of tension between what actually is on the one hand and what ought to be on the other hand. Hence the more a person identifies the self with the state of things as they are, the more it eliminates distance from the person and forfeits the fruitful tension between *what is* and *what ought to be*. Thus within suffering a person experiences wisdom greater than reason, and counter to our own logical rationality; it is within the tension that life is given perspective to find the greater meanings of one's very existence.

Frankl points out exactly what this fruitful tension is, for while some complain that life swings between distress and tedium. In reality both have their own meaning. Monotony is a continual reminder to avoid inactivity. But action does not exist for the purpose of evading boredom; rather, boredom exists so that we will flee it, and do justice to the meaning of our life. The tensions of life keep us in anticipation because the meaning of life depends upon how we respond to the demands placed upon us.[14]

The Doctor and the Soul highlights the importance of attitude toward life's tensions. Within life, suffering reveals a tension, for all people will suffer in some form. Suffering can reveal a twofold meaning: it can help shape the person, where possible; and help the person to choose an attitude in order to endure the suffering where necessary. Life is opportunities. Equally, suffering can be an opportunity for greatness. A person suffering an unchangeable fate, and meeting it with tranquility, is a hero.[15]

Logotherapy is about doing; that is choosing an action. This makes sense when remembering the principle of meaning as an experience revealed through a response to life. When a person is responsible to life, life reveals meaning. Logotherapy calls for a person to act, for the language of life is action. Life asks the person about the meaning of this life, a person's response should be by doing. a person's response should be by doing. Of course, the correct response depends upon the situation, the person, and the context. Life gives the person a context to experience a value. The person makes a responsible reply and then experiences meaning. The person chooses an action in response to life's demands, and maybe even changes the conditions of life.[16]

Here the expression of creative values is at the forefront of the meaning of work. Work is typically the place where a person expresses uniqueness in society and thus receives meaning and value. This meaning and value is attached to the person's actions, not occupation. Therefore, no particular occupation offers a person the opportunity for total fulfillment. Moreover, it is the action, not occupation exclusively, that provides meaning in a person's life. Personal actions, such as being a lover or being loved, also provide meaning.[17]

Meaning reveals itself within living values, even in the presence of suffering. Meaning in the presence of suffering provides the person strength to deal with the situation. An active, engaged, living response to life's situations always reveals meaning. Yet the question remains how to enact these principles in the psychotherapeutic relationship. To this end, we now turn to the praxis of Logotherapy.

LOGOTHERAPY PRAXIS

Frankl did not consider Logotherapy to be a new distinctive approach, so much as an adjunct and a call for rehumanizing psychiatry. However, as a psychotherapeutic approach, it does have a few important techniques within its repertoire. The first of these techniques is that of *paradoxical intention.* This is a particularly good treatment of anticipatory anxiety. For this anxiety, often produces that situation the patient fears. This fear of fear may arise for several reasons. The fear of collapse due to a panic attack. The fear of a heart attack that raises anxiety and the risk of an actual episode. The fear that a panic attack will cause some kind of brain damage. Overall, this fear of fear expresses itself within patients as pathological avoidance patterns of response.[18]

Anticipatory anxiety often brings about the feared result through excessive attention. What Frankl calls *hyper-intention.* This hyper-intention prevents the patient from living with a sense of peace. One logotherapeutic response is the technique of paradoxical intention. The phobic patient, "is invited to intend, even if only for a moment, precisely that which he fears."[19]

Another technique known as *de-reflection* takes the logical counter to the hyper-reflection. Hyper-reflection focuses on some performance goal; *de-reflection* moves the attention away from this performance goal. De-reflection often applies to treating male sexual dysfunctions, like erectile dysfunction. Often, the hyper-intention on sexual performance results in a placid penis. By de-reflecting *from* performance *to* attention on the partner, the problem disappears.

In summary, *paradoxical intention* counters anticipatory *anxiety*. So too, *de-reflection* counters a compulsive inclination to *self-observation.* Through paradoxical intention, the patient tries to ridicule the symptoms, while learning to ignore them through de-reflection.[20] Logotherapy applies paradoxical intention and de-reflection to counter basic neurotic patterns. When the patient uses withdrawal and avoidance patterns, Logotherapy uses paradoxical intention by helping the patient ridicule the symptoms. When the patient uses wrong activity, fighting against obsessive ideas, Logotherapy replaces this with right activity. Here de-reflection helps the patient ignore the neurosis of self-assessment and focus attention on the care of others.

ANALYSIS OF RESPONSIBILITY

Logotherapy believes that psychotherapy needs supplementing with a means to positively engage the spiritual sphere. The guiding principles for Logotherapy and existential analysis do this by engaging *responsibleness.*

Existential analysis lays weight on the all-inclusive quality of existence. For feeling existence profoundly, within an attitude of responsibility, starts a process of growth. In this Logotherapy seeks to fills the gap that traditional psychotherapy ignores.[21]

As Frankl points out, the aim of psychotherapy, especially psychoanalysis, is toward what he calls a *secular confession*. Logotherapy, by contrast, recognizes that there is a spiritual part of life and that struggles are inevitable. As such Logotherapy, existential analysis, and medical ministry engage the person where psychotherapy fails. Now, of course, Frankl is adamant that Logotherapy is not religious, nor does it seek to replace the clergy or pastoral ministry; rather, it seeks to help those people that need a hand engaging the spiritual and meaning components of life.[22] In such a way, Logotherapy provides a means for the therapist to engage the full humanness of the client. It is a place to engage the spiritual dimension within psychotherapy. It is a means for respecting for the full humanity of the client.

SUMMARY

Frankl sees psychotherapy as being blind to the higher dimensions of a person. For Frankl, spirituality is part of an accurate picture of a person. A person is a human being who is full of meaning. To ignore the humanness of a person is to make psychotherapy far too narrow and shallow. Within this human dimension, Logotherapy identifies two great treasures of humans. The first is the human capacity for self-detachment, to endure despite circumstances. The second is the human capacity for self-transcendence.

According to Frankl, people are outward existential beings who engage outside of themselves to be fully conscious and human. This takes expression in moving toward something or someone other than the self. People move toward meanings to fulfill. The more people live out self-transcendence, the more human they become. Therefore, psychotherapy must value self-transcendence as part of the human experience.[23]

Furthermore, people have the capacity to operate with a reason and meaning. This has powerful therapeutic value, for there will be suffering, loss, and even death in the lives of every person. Yet meaning may be wrung out of every experience, bringing comfort and strength. So psychotherapy should have the capacity to engage these sources of encouragement and resilience.

Ultimately, Frankl's first book, *The Doctor and the Soul*, and the rise of Logotherapy are about the very nature of humanity. The goal of Logotherapy is to help the psychiatric profession reclaim the humanness of patients. Pleasure alone will never satisfy a person, for death shows this to be empty, as in death pleasure vanishes. Yet a person desires meaning and happiness, always struggling with the vexing problem of how to find them. For Frankl, this desire for meaning and happiness ties in with values. Values reside outside the self and actualize in actions and experiences. Through this, a person experiences meaning and a different kind of happiness, namely joy. So, in a sense, Logotherapy is about how people can ultimately experience joy.

Frankl sees joy as a natural side benefit of Logotherapy, as something that occurs with self-transcendence. Unlike pleasure, joy is never an end in itself. It springs spontaneously from forgetting the self in the other. As Frankl likes to point out, the door to happiness opens outward. Anyone who tries to pull open the door simply closes it more firmly. This intentional self-transcendent nature of people is what Logotherapy tries to honor. As Frankl says at the conclusion of *The Doctor and the Soul*, "For too long the cry [for meaning] has remained unheard. But a psychotherapy that sets out on its way to rehumanization should listen to the unheard cry for meaning."[24]

NOTES

1. Frankl, *Man's Search for Meaning*, 113.
2. Viktor Frankl, *The Doctor and the Soul* (New York: Vintage Books, 1986), x.
3. Ibid., xi.
4. Ibid., x.
5. Frankl, *Recollections*, 104–106.
6. Frankl, *The Doctor and the Soul*, xvii.
7. Ibid.
8. Ibid., 7.
9. Ibid., 33.
10. According to Frankl, *The Doctor and the Soul*, 33: The world appears to manifest something akin to a law of the conservation of spiritual energy. No great idea can vanish, even if it never reaches public circulation, even if it has been "taken to the grave." In the light of such a law, the drama and tragedy of a man's inner life never have unfolded in vain, even when played out in secret, unrecorded, uncelebrated by any novelist. The "novel" which each individual has lived remains an incomparably greater composition than any that has ever been written down. Every one of us knows somehow that the content of his life is somewhere preserved and saved. Thus time, the transitoriness of the years, cannot affect its meaning and value. Having been is a kind of being – perhaps the surest kind. And all effective action in life may, in this view, appear as a salvaging of possibilities by actualizing them. Though past, these possibilities are now safely ensconced in the past for all eternity, and time can no longer change them.
11. Ibid., 71.
12. Frankl points out that experiencing meaning in suffering is possible, and can be a centrally important skill in a person's life: "The destiny a person suffers therefore has a twofold meaning: to be shaped where possible, and to be endured where

necessary. Let us also remember that "inactive," passive enduring still retains the immanent meaning of all suffering. On the other hand, man must be on his guard against the temptation to lay down his arms prematurely, too soon accepting a state of things as destined and bowing his head before a merely imaginary fate. Only when he no longer has any possibility of actualizing creative values, when there is really no means at hand for shaping fate – then is the time for attitudinal values to be actualized; then alone does it have meaning for him to "take his cross." The very essence of an attitudinal value inheres in the manner in which a person resigns himself to must be actually inevitable. It must be what Brod has called "noble misfortune" as against the "ignoble misfortune," the latter being something which is either avoidable, or for which the person himself is to blame." Frankl, *The Doctor and the Soul,* 111–112.

13. Ibid., 56.
14. Frankl, *The Doctor and the Soul*, 109.
15. Ibid., 116.
16. According to Frankl, within that area, every man is indispensable and irreplaceable. We have already discussed the importance of the individual's being conscious of his uniqueness and singularity. We have seen the reasons why existential analysis works toward bringing responsibility to consciousness, and how consciousness of responsibility arises above all out of awareness of a concrete personal task: a "mission." Without perception of the unique meaning of his singular existence, a person would be numbed in difficult situations. He would be like the mountain climber who enters a dense fog and, lacking the goal before his eyes, is in danger of succumbing to a total weariness. If the fog lifts and he catches sight of the shelter hut in the distance, he at once feels a renewed strength. Every climber has experienced fatigue, the flagging energy that attacks him when he is "in the wall" and cannot tell whether he may not be taking a wrong route, whether he has not perhaps entered a blind crevice – until suddenly he sees the escape chimney. Then, realizing that he is only a few rope lengths below the peak, he feels fresh strength coursing into his arms as he reaches out cheerfully for new holds. Frankl, *The Doctor and the Soul*, 117–118.
17. Frankl, *The Doctor and the Soul*, 127–128.
18. Ibid., 222–223.
19. Ibid., 223.
20. Ibid., 255.
21. Ibid., 273.
22. Ibid., 275–276.
23. Ibid., 295.
24. Ibid., 301.

Chapter 4

Frankl's Existential Anthropology

A DIMENSIONAL ONTOLOGY

In response to the failures of the psychotherapy of his day, Frankl believed it is important to define an anthropology that incorporates spirituality. The result was a robust philosophical anthropology. Existential phenomenology and the hermeneutical capacity of patients were two key areas incorporated by Frankl. He clearly affirms the features that make us human and advances to build therapy on them. Through Logotherapy, he seeks to reveal a worldview sufficient for dealing with the tension between human experience and psychiatric reductionism.[1] This chapter will explore Frankl's existential anthropology, beginning with his emphasis upon the whole person. We will also consider the importance of love, freedom, will, meaning, and mortality.[2]

A UNIFIED DIMENSIONALISM

Frankl's view of people is multidimensional. He responds to the scientific reductionism that dehumanizes the patient.[3] He claims that a few select causes cannot bring about a true understanding of infinitely complex beings. In particular, he criticizes Freudianism for reducing people to pure biology.[4] In Frankl's view, this degrades the person to a series of dynamics and allows the therapist to view of the patient in subhuman terms.

Frankl views his own anthropology as being counter-scientific.[5] Counter, not in denying scientific observations, but by countering the narrow view of reductionism. He wishes to offset and neutralize the dehumanizing effects that follow reductionism. He always frames his own understanding of human nature, trying to consider multiple perspectives.[6] Therefore, Frankl argues for a trans-dimensional view of humanity.

Frankl argues that reductionism leads to an implicit determinism that fails in understanding the person. People transcend drives or intrapsychic conflicts. For humans operate on many different levels simultaneously. Therefore, while the schools of Psychoanalysis, Individual Psychology, and Behaviorism all have something to contribute; each is only a small portion of a fuller reality.[7]

Frankl takes a practical approach to the reductionism within psychiatry. Continually making the point that he was not wishing to directly oppose or contradict the findings of psycho analysts or behaviorists. Rather, he wishes to add to them, for their restricted scope leads to an incomplete understanding of how to help people. People long for meaning. It is erroneous to think a person is *nothing but* psychodynamics or conditioned responses. Frankl argues that traditional psychotherapy seems to argue that if you only get rid of your defense mechanisms that people will become all they can be. Frankl mocks this authoritarian view of traditional psychotherapy by saying, "Doesn't it sound somewhat like, Seek ye first the kingdom of Freud and Skinner, and all these things will be added unto you?"[8]

Frankl seeks to solve the enigma of a therapeutic anthropology while honoring the wholeness of the person. This requires a complicated vocabulary for a difficult problem. Eventually he comes up with the term "dimensional ontology."[9] Any accurate reduction of people, to a single dimension, isn't possible. Rather, any talk of a specific dimension must imply the presence of all other human dimensions. Be they physical, psychological, or spiritual. For Frankl, one might rightly speak of determinism in the bio-psychological dimension, and autonomy in the noological dimension. The dimensional paradigm of understanding people means that there tensions can exist within a person, for there is unity and also diversity within a person. So when considering the free choice within a person, Frankl would use the phrase, "Freedom in spite of determinism."[10]

This is not to deny the influence of other causes, for Frankl is, "fully aware of the extent to which man is subject to biological, psychological, and sociological conditions."[11] What concerns him is psychiatry's tendency to engage in "*regressus in infinitum.*"[12,13] Where therapists become fatalistic that discount any role of the human dimension whatsoever. At the same time, Frankl recognizes that there are factors that influence people's experiences. Noting for instance, that paranoia or endogeneous depression have an etiology that is somatic and biochemical. Yet, he notes, "We are not justified in making fatalistic inferences."[14]

In so doing Frankl draws from existentialism to define his anthropology as a dimensionalism that must include the power of choice. He points out that people are not naked apes nor machines, nor computers. Each analogy fails to grasp the human dimensional difference essential to understand people. This dimensional difference is the power of choice lost in reductionism.

Frankl also dislikes the standard scientific view of people, as it ignores meaning. Meaning is missing in the world as depicted by many a science, but for Frankl this is simply evidence that many a science is blind to it. In Frankl's view, we must not reduce people to deterministic creatures. Rather, people are complex beings that live within the intersection of myriad meanings. The therapist must honor people as such, even though the more complete the meaning, the less graspable it is. This ultimately necessitates an attitude of unknowing on the part of the therapist.

Within all of this then Frankl admits that humanity is on one level animal, while simultaneously "infinitely surpasses his animal properties."[15] In this sense then there is a noetic dimension that defines what it means to be human. According to Frankl, the noological dimension is distinct from the biological and psychological dimensions. It is the dimension that makes humanity unique, and where the greatness of human potential lies.[16]

> Man passes the noological dimension[17] whenever he is reflecting upon himself – or, if need be, rejecting himself; whenever he is making himself an object – or making objections to himself; whenever he displays his being conscious of himself – or whenever he exhibits his being conscientious. In fact, being conscientious presupposes the uniquely human capacity to rise above oneself, to judge and evaluate one's own deeds in moral or ethical terms.[18]

In summary, Frankl is clearly not a philosophical materialist who reduces the person to one dimension or another. Rather in his view the person is a unified being with multiple unified dimensions. Frankl does not reduce the brain to mere physical matter, nor does he define the mind as simply the brain. Rather the human mind is both physical and immaterial and spiritual. The mind is body and also transcends the body. In this way people are capable of rising above the conditions of their biological, psychological, or social environment to become something more. In short, people are Spirit.

It is within this vein that Frankl points to the next important area that helps us understand his anthropology. Frankl considers the quality of love to be a most excellent example of the noological dimension. Therefore to truly understand people, one must understand how people love. Within this, Frankl asserts, we find the "striking manifestation of another uniquely human capacity, the capacity of self-transcendence." This quality of love, of course, hinges on his principle of a unified dimensionalism. This is counter to the reductionism of love, namely sex and the pleasure principle.

LOVE AS A HUMAN QUALITY

Frankl views love as a capacity within humanity that helps define people. People have the capacity to discover meaning through love. Love recognizes the unique value of every person as irreplaceable. Love reveals a layer of being where every person is special, not a group, or comparable, nor replaceable. Love reveals a person as possessing the dignity of personal uniqueness. "This dignity is the dignity of those angels of whom some scholastics maintained that they do not represent a kind; rather, there is only one of each kind."[19]

Remembering the wholeness of existence is always essential. Frankl is aware that scientific reductionism often interprets love in the *nothing but* sense of sexuality. In response to this, Frankl retorts that actually love could not be just the result of the sublimation of sex because, whenever sublimation takes place, love has been the precondition. Thus, Frankl makes distinct the capacity for love and the sexual instinct, though sexuality may still be an expression of love.

Frankl interprets mature human love as something greater than sexual drives and sublimation tendencies. It isn't simply a side effect of sex; rather, sex is a means of expressing the experience of togetherness within love.[20] In this, Frankl accepts that sex is of love, but clarifies that sex is not uniquely human but is of a lower, more animal form. This fits well with his view of human dimensionality, while insisting on unity. In this then Frankl points out there is within the human capacity, an animal attitude of love that is sexual in nature: "The most primitive attitude concerns itself with the outermost layer: This is the sexual attitude."[21]

Overall, Frankl views human capacity of love as something higher than sexuality. Human love may experience another person in uniqueness.[22] Human love becomes a defining feature of people. People have the ability to seize the individual as unique, and to extend grace. So, human love exists in the act of loving, and being loved.[23]

This view of love provides a glimpse into the intersubjectivity of love. For Frankl, objectifying a person is to devalue that person. The value of a person lies in the person's uniqueness, and subjective uniqueness is what makes love possible. Human love knows the other in personhood.[24] Yet human love goes deeper still. True love goes beyond mere personality traits or peculiarities of the person, for these are subject to change. Love commitments to care, monogamy, and binds the beloved and lover. Such real love, and it alone leads to a monogamous attitude. Monogamous love commits to the partner, beyond what is common in people.[25]

This commitment points to the self-transcendence of human love. For neither power nor pleasure moves spiritual love. Rather this love reveals meaning and further strengthens itself by reinforcing the self-transcendent love for the other. This reveals the unique capacity of human love. For human love, through self-transcendence, reveals happiness as a by-product.[26] Mature love means the higher dimensions unify the lower dimensions within them.

Frankl makes it clear that the self-transcendent quality of love is a key ingredient in his anthropology. It denotes the fact that being human means being in relationship with, and being directed to the care of someone other than oneself. This forms a staple of Logotherapy that existence is dependent upon the human aspect of self-transcendence. Every human thought is drawn in relationship, from something, to something and pointed to something or someone. Meaning then is encountered in concern for the other, in actions to serve or love a person. It is in living out this self-transcendence then, that people become fully human.

When love is expressed in self-transcendent qualities, it incorporates the various dimensions of the person. It may be sexual, but it is much more than mere sexuality. It is a grasping of the other, an apprehension of the meaning, a commitment to the other, and in that way the lover becomes fully human. Thereby sexuality is redeemed and made human by the experience of meaning in the self-transcendent love of the uniqueness of the other. Sex becomes human only as a result of a process where the other is engaged on the human noological level. Sex is human when the uniqueness of the person is honored, and this comes through love.

In summary, for Frankl, mature self-transcendent love is a defining quality of human existence. Fully human love is an existential act that reveals meaning for existence. The roots of love move from the emotional and intuitive, nonrational depths of the spiritual unconscious where meaning reveals itself to the soul. Love is human in committing to and understands the uniqueness of the other, revealing meaning for both beloved and lover. Love is fully human within self-transcendence, and it is here where we experience deep happiness. Love is choosing to commitment to care of the other. This choosing aspect of love reveals the importance of another key to Frankl's anthropology, the will.

FREEDOM OF THE WILL

A discussion of Frankl's anthropology isn't complete without exploring his concept of *freedom of the will*. This is a crucial feature for understanding humanity for "Freedom is not something we 'have' and therefore can lose; freedom is what we 'are.'"[27] Frankl draws from Jean-Paul Sartre while defining freedom in his own way and not simply buying into Sartre's extreme existential philosophy.

To better understand Frankl's view, it is helpful to explore Sartre's existential perspective. For Sartre, an essential part of *being* is *nothingness*: the negation of things experienced or expected.[28] Second, Sartre sees the absolute freedom of humanity as its defining feature.[29]

This freedom is the ability to define the self through the ever-present need to make choices. In this Sartre puts forward two great ideas: First is *people are condemned to be free*; second is *existence precedes essence*. In both, Sartre gives expression to human freedom and the need to make choices. There are great implications of Sartre's philosophy. That is, people have no essential quality; *no essences of people* are foundational – save, intentionality. It is a person's *choices and attitudes* that define a person's essence.[30]

Sartre and Frankl agree the *freedom of the will* is central to understanding people. Frankl holds that choice must be understood within the limits of circumstances. This is in contrast to an all-inclusive, self-creating choice of Sartre's extreme view. Yet, even within these limits of circumstances, Frankl does recognize the power of human spirituality, for spirituality allows people to make choices that transcend horrible circumstances.[31]

While Frankl agrees with Sartre on the importance of the freedom of the will, he takes a different direction. For Sartre, freedom of the will leads to the issue of absurdity; for if the foundation of a person's essence is choices and attitudes, then this must also be the source of any meaning within life.[32] If this is the source of any meaning in life, then humanity is the source of all meaning. According to this line of thinking, the absurdity of human existence is the necessary result of our attempts to live a life of meaning and purpose within an inanimate cosmos.[33] This is something that Frankl rejects, for meaning must not coincide with being, but meaning must precede being. Meaning sets the context for being, and being reveals meaning. Existence falters except in transcendence toward something beyond itself.[34]

The essence of Sartre's view of humanity is that people are beings of whom no essence can be affirmed – for such an essence introduces a permanent element, contradictory to the power of transforming the self indefinitely. In this, Sartre points out that people are condemned to be free. He defines human experience along two basic premises: Existence precedes essence; and the world is organized into two types of being: *Being in itself* and the *Being for itself*.[35] As Lavine makes clear, the freedom of humanity according to Sartre has profound consequences:

> In Jean-Paul Sartre's novel *The Age of Reason* (1945), his hero . . . proclaims Sartre's philosophy of human freedom: He was free, free for everything, free to act like an animal or like a machine. . . . He could do what he wanted to do, nobody had the right to advise him. . . . He alone in a monstrous silence, free and alone, without an excuse, condemned to decide without an excuse, condemned to decide without any possible recourse, condemned forever to be free.[36]

In understanding Sartre's view that we are *condemned to be free* we must grasp that *existence precedes essence* and therefore Sartre's atheism. Sartre's analogy is that when an artisan creates an object, such an object simply exists with an inbuilt essence. This essence or nature determines its life and consequently it is not free to act otherwise. This ties into Sartre's atheism, as he views God as a supernatural artisan, and following his logic if we are created then a person's essence has been determined. In a way then, Sartre's insistence that existence precedes essence is a counter to Leibniz view. For Liebniz believes God fixes each person's essence, and then leaves each person to act freely following the demands of this essence.[37]

For Sartre, Leibniz description of freedom is no freedom at all. If we are the product of a creative God, then the one original gesture decides existence. For Sartre, we are without any preestablished pattern for human nature; each person makes essence in living. Sartre's classification then to his understanding of being as, *being in itself* which is the being of things. Like the product of the artisan. These objects are not responsible. They have a determined essence and cannot, by their own will, alter from it. In contrast, people are not fixed and complete, and exist as *being for itself* – that is, being conscious, responsible, and free.[38]

This lack of an essence is something that Frankl challenges. Frankl views humanity as a being of vast, almost unfathomable potential, but still fixed by the divine. This view of the divine means that Frankl's view is more in line with Leibniz's than Sartre's. For with God, there is a context for human existence. God imbues existence with meaning, providing a context for being human. In taking this view, Frankl rejects Sartre's notion that man can choose and design himself without a foundation. In fact, Frankl calls Sartre's view that existence is total freedom, an illusion, similar to the fakir trick where a fakir throws a rope into the air and attempts to climb the rope.[39]

For Sartre, man is nothing else but what he makes of himself. Such is the first principle of existentialism that he sets forth in his lecture on *Existentialism is a Humanism*:

> Man is at the start a plan which is aware of itself . . . but if existence really does precede essence, man is responsible for what he is. Thus, existentialism's first move is to make every man aware of what he is and to make the full responsibility of his existence rest on him. And when we say that a man is responsible for himself, we do not only mean that he is responsible for his own individuality, but that he is responsible for all men. . . . That is the idea I shall try to convey when I say that man is condemned to be free. Condemned, because he did not create himself, yet, in other respects is free; because once thrown into the world, he is responsible for everything he does. . . . He thinks that man is responsible for his passion.[40]

It should be noted here that this extreme viewpoint that people are *nothing but*, was something that Frankl vehemently denies. Whether in discussion with his secondary school science teacher, Sartre, or Freud, Frankl always insists that humanity can never be simply reduced. Frankl is determined to find a balance. He avoids a determinism where we have no choice, and a nihilism where we are condemned by our freedom. Frankl argued that people buy into determinism or nihilism simply because people have difficulty distinguishing between causes and conditions.

Frankl recognizes the freedom of the will as an essential feature of people. It is not an absolute freedom, but a freedom within limits. People are subject to conditions, whether they are biological, psychological, or social factors. Yet, people are free to stand against these conditions, even if only through an attitude chosen. This rebellion affirms the essential freedom within people.

Further, Frankl views people not as one thing among others, where things are determining each other. Rather he recognizes that people are self-determining, within the limits of finitude, at which point freedom is restricted. Given this supreme limit, within the bounds of this limit humanity has a responsibility to exercise freedom. This freedom and responsibility balance helps to define people, and is where meaning reveals itself in being.

THE EXPERIENCE OF MEANING

In Frankl's view of the freedom of choice is a modified constructivist sense. The key difference between Frankl's existential view and that of Sartre is that Frankl considers meaning to be already imbedded within reality. Whereas Sartre views meaning as something created with the self, as its sole source and authority. For Frankl, the meaning is already present within reality. This allows Frankl to avoid the problem of nihilism and ultimate meaninglessness that results from a pure constructivism. For Frankl the question is: How can a person make choices that will reveal the meaning that is already present? How can a person live out this meaning imbued existence?

Frankl makes an allusion to God's leading the Israelite people out of Egypt in the biblical Exodus, illustrating the tentative and journey-like nature of living a meaningful life. The Israelites did not know exactly where the end-goal was from day to day or week to week. Instead they followed the guidance of God in the form a cloud, with the *promised land* being the goal that energized each day of living in the wilderness.[41] As Frankl states, "To direct one's life toward a goal is of vital importance."[42]

Just as the Israelite experience of traveling out of Egypt and living in the wilderness, so too, Frankl considers a meaningful life to be one of engagement and activity. Yet, there is always a higher and less clear meaning that, like the divine cloud, provides a context for that meaning and accountability for the daily choices of engagement. In such a way, a person's entire life is a dynamic discovery process of meaning within life.[43]

Like all existentialists, Frankl deals with the problem of meaning and the personal answer that will help people to understand existence. The question is: Does life as a whole have meaning, or is it meaningless?[44] In working through this question one can be tempted by some philosophers to conclude that life is nothing but a mass of nonsense and a reduction of things smaller. To this, Frankl responds with his unified dimensionalism,[45] rejecting reductionism as an ultimate answer. The conclusion that Frankl arrives at is that there is meaning within life, but there are limits to our apprehension of that meaning:

> [There is an ultimate meaning] that is "up to heaven," . . . some sort of ultimate meaning, that is; a meaning of the whole, of the "universe," or at least a meaning of one's life as a whole; . . . a long range meaning. . . . To invoke an analogy, consider a movie: It consists of thousands upon thousands of individual pictures, and each of them makes sense and carries a meaning, yet the meaning of the whole film cannot be seen before its last sequence is shown. On the other hand, we cannot understand the whole film without having first understood each of its components, each of the individual pictures. Isn't it the same with life?[46]

Meaning may at times appear meaningless because we fail to grasp the ultimate meaning. This however is not because there is no ultimate meaning. Rather it has to do with the fact that we are limited in our capacity, and so the problem of existence will never be fully solved by people. All being is ambiguous, and in the absence of clarity it is tempting to conclude that existence is either meaningless, nonsense, or is an unknowable ultimate reality. In response to these temptations, Frankl falls back on the present existence of the individual facing these problems. A person is always left to choose; and the choice ought to be informed by a Kierkegaardian leap of faith. As Frankl says, in reflecting upon his experiences in the Nazi camps, "The prisoner who had lost faith in the future – his future – was doomed. With his loss of belief in the future, he also lost his spiritual hold; he let himself decline and . . . decay."[47] With this leap of faith, we choose to believe and incorporate into our thinking the recognition that the meaningfulness of reality extends beyond our own human limits, providing hope for our future. What a person is left with then, according to Frankl, is the choice to live in responsibility: "Each life situation confronting us places a demand on us, presents a question to us – a question to which we have to answer by doing something about the given situation."[48]

When living in this responsibility then, people will begin to experience meaning. In this way people give an existential answer to an existential question by living the answer. People then experience the meaning pre-reflectively.

It is when the person then reflects upon the meaning of the life lived, that the meaning of life begins to resolve and coalesce into clarity. As a person evaluates a lived life, with the perspective on the past, the present, and a hope for *promised-land* future, the meaning of life becomes clear.

Here again we see just how important Frankl's *unified dimensionalism* is to this approach to meaning. We are fully embodied beings, not just a mind. Therefore we cannot fully experience meaning by simply philosophizing upon the existential question of the meaning of life. We are beings that exist in the physical level, the relational level, the psychological level, and the spiritual level, to name but a few. As such Frankl insists that in order to actualize meaning in experience. We must reach beyond ourselves and transcend the self, to love and care for something or someone other than the self. By the same token, Frankl argues that our existence cannot consist of self-actualization; that our main goal cannot be in making ourselves and fulfilling our own needs. For in so doing, we are not truly choosing to engage the dynamic external world and caring for it. Rather, we reveal and experience meaning only when we truly engage the world. For meaning is not created from within, but discovered in the world.

So meaning is discovered in the pre-reflective frame of our existence when we engage fully in choices for the care and love of something within the world, outside of the self. This meaning is then drawn into a more conscious, reflective frame of experience where we are able to step back in quiet contemplation to organize these experiences and discover a coherent meaningful narrative. Within all of this then, there is a tension that exists in the living of a meaningful life. Frankl frames this tension as *noodynamics*[49] and considers it a balance of appropriate tension that must exist to hold us steady toward actualizing concrete values, which have the benefit of infusing our existence with meaning.

Noodynamics is, for Frankl, the constant tension between who we are in our present life, and our potential or our ideal self. This tension is intrinsic in being human and hence indispensable for mental well-being.[50] It is a tension between our existence and essence, our choices, our goals, our wishes, and our weaknesses, between our meaning and our being. Meaning is always before being, but it is not fully experienced until we actualize it in choices we make within the world. So we experience meaning in the choices we make within the world, not within some inner intrapsychic drive.

In this way then, Frankl's principles of unified dimensionalism, love, and freedom of the will are all essential for the problem of meaning and meaningless. A meaningful life requires the choice of living out love within the world. When any component is missing, meaning does not reveal itself in the experience. The result, we feel meaningless. Hence, Frankl points to existential dynamics at work within existence. For we live along a continuum of success and failure.

Frankl contends that true satisfaction comes, not when a reward is given, like money; but when something meaningful has been done. In line with this principle of existential dynamics then, it is possible to realize meaning, success, and satisfaction even in uncomfortable or difficult conditions. As Frankl said, "Man is ready and willing to shoulder any suffering as soon as long as he can see a meaning in it."[51] Meaning, therefore, is not only essential for true success but is also essential for resiliency within life. For suffering without meaning is despair which is unbearable, but suffering with meaning raises man above despair and provides courage to survive in the face of suffering.

In summary then, Frankl was clear that one might enjoy a long, full life of pleasure and power and still suffer the despair of meaninglessness. For without love to actualize in choices, meaning does not reveal itself in experience. A life lived in the pursuit of pleasure and power fails to reveal meaning to the pre-reflective experiences of a person. The reflective self requires this pre-reflective experience to then draw up a meaning of life. Conversely, it is possible that one has to face a situation that is full of discomfort and weakness, and yet still operates within choices that actualize love: "Be it for the sake of a cause to which we are committed; be it for a loved one, or for the sake of God."[52] This choice to actualize love in the world then brings the experience of meaning to life, even when power and pleasure are absent.

MORTALITY

The life challenge facing all existential thinkers is the problem of *Death*. The issue of death is one of the foundational existential problems that make up existential psychotherapy in general. People long to free themselves of the uneasy awareness of death. Yet, life awakens apprehension, and so a tension exists within every person. Within each person is the deep, ever-present anxiety of death framing life. Yet, there is the need to risk death in living. Overall then, the genuine life means finding the tension between engaging life and accepting the transitory nature of existence. The irony then is that death, in many ways, can save life. This occurs by helping the person to recognize the importance of every choice within existence.

Frankl views death as expressing the impermanence of life, and not as some barrier to conquer. If we look closely at life we see that every moment, from activities to time itself, reminds us of our eventual death. The awareness of our mortality is a specifically human capacity, according to Frankl, and this awareness helps us to appreciate life or despair because of it. For the pessimist observes with fear and dread as the days of life tick away, and death draws ever closer. In contrast, Frankl sees the optimistic response to death to be based upon life already lived, and meanings already discovered through the actualizing of love.

Frankl turns the fear of death on its head, for things that seem to take meaning from human life belong with it. This includes issues of death, suffering, and also the whole nature of the potentialities of life. We should recognize the only transitory quality of life is its potentialities. The moment we actualize experience in action, potentialities move from possibilities to realities. In Frankl's view then, living life redeems life, even in the face of death. The past is a secure storehouse that death cannot penetrate.[53]

Within this we see that Frankl's view relies upon a security of the past, through the actualized values within life. Life then exists despite death, and nothing can take away the valuable things that a man does for they already exist in the past. Every task that we fulfill, every love chosen, is part of the eternity of the past and makes up life, in quality and meaning. The importance of the actualizing nature of human life provides a context for meaning, challenging the often accepted notion that death somehow nullifies a life lived.[54]

In summary then, death is simply the end of opportunities to actualize possibilities. Yet, Frankl's view of meaning permeating reality does leave open the possibility for something unknown beyond death. Death is not a cancellation of meaning; it is the point where the summary meaning of life is written into the past. "What about death – does it not completely cancel the meaning of our life? By no means. As the end belongs to the story, so death belongs to life."[55] As a person dies, the person creates the self, even up to the very moment of death. The self is not something that is static, it is always moving beyond itself. The self is always becoming, and therefore becomes itself fully only when life has been completed in death.

SUMMARY

Frankl holds a complex and intricate existential anthropology that forms the basis for his logotherapeutic approach. Each piece has an important role to play in living the meaningful life. This also helps guide the therapist in helping the patient, and ensures a logical consistency to the overall meaningful human experience.

Frankl claims that defining people by one or two dimensions dehumanizes them. He pushes for a concept where each dimension incorporates those below it. Furthermore, he believes three basic essential qualities must remain coalesced: the body (soma), the mind (psyche), and the spirit (noos). Each dimension intertwines with the others and affords an understanding of people as unified whole.

Love is a key unifying force for understanding the uniqueness of people. Love is the meaning before the action, and when actualized, reveals the meaning hidden within the world. Love is uniquely human. Love is also a key to an authentic human existence. Love is intuitive and emerges in the emotional, intellectual, and spiritual being of a person. Love is so important that it is vital for therapy to nurture the actualizing of a mature love within life. Implicit in this is the self-transcendent nature of love, where one forgets oneself in the service of something, or someone other than the self. Love is intentional, directing outward into the world and actualized within the world. Love, is intentional action. Real love, in Frankl's theory, is concerned for the well-being of the other; and suffering may be chosen for the sake of the care of the other.

According to Frankl, fate does not determine or define people. To apply deterministic laws of causality upon people dehumanizes. Despite internal psychic drives, genetic limitations, and influences of the environment, people are still free in the choice. While people can never declare freedom from causal links, we are always free to transcend them toward a meaningful goal within life. This ability of the will then implies that action is not only possible, but necessary in living out existence. In every moment we make a choice to one direction or another. The sign of a mature, authentic person is one who chooses what is responsible. Choosing, despite barriers, to enact a meaning within life through the transcendence of the self in the service of love and care for someone or something other than the self.

In the expression of the freedom of the will, meaning reveals itself. Love brings meaning into view, and so people have the opportunity to experience happiness. Whether people are pursuing happiness or meaning, the experience of happiness will never be reached unless one commits to enacting the meaning in love. According to Frankl, there is continuity within the experience of meaning, for it is impracticable to separate the meaning of the moment from the meaning of the whole. As the meaning of the whole cannot be contrived, so is it also hopeless to simply conjure from imagination concrete meanings and the meaning content of one's life. Meanings have to be discovered from among the number of potentialities that a person experiences. True meanings are ones that fit into the higher meanings, the meanings of experience, and are revealed through the conscience.

Frankl views death as a key part of life. It is an experience that serves to summarize one's personal meaning of life. Death is essentially the closing of opportunities. Death is not an annulment of meaning, but the crux where the summary meaning of one's life is written into the past. In a sense then, death saves life by creating a context for each choice, ensuring that each choice we make within life is important.

Within this well-developed framework for understanding humanity, Frankl is able to create a context for allowing the meaning component of life to be explored within the therapist's office. This framework also allows Frankl to continue to engage in his work tirelessly. He was a resilient man, working well past the retirement age, continually teaching and writing about his approach of Logotherapy. Within the final chapter, we will explore Frankl's swan song and his legacy within psychotherapy.

NOTES

1. "Reductionism" is a term that refers to the theory that all psychological processes follow biological principles and all biological processes follow the same laws as chemistry and physics. According to Neil Wollman "Jung and Freud compared on two types of reductionism," *Journal of Analytical Psychology*, 27, (1982), 149–161 the primary type of reductionism that main stream Freudian psychiatry followed was a Lockean reductionism that states that complex levels of consciousness are composed of and can be reduced to more basic abstract units. In addition to this is a narrower type of substrate reductionism that reduces the phenomenon to something of a totally different nature, positing an explanation in terms of a qualitatively different structure, such as biological drives and sexuality.

2. According to Yalom's *Existential Psychotherapy*, 14–15 Existentialism is not easily definable, but he points out most existential writers deal with problems relating to existence that include being, choice, freedom, death, isolation, and absurdity. Within this chapter we will explore how Frankl implicitly deals with these themes, while using the language that best suits Frankl. As such the sections entitled "Unified Dimensionalism" and "Love as a Uniquely Human Capacity" will provide a general framework for Frankl's view of Being. Choice and freedom will be dealt with in the section entitled "Freedom of the Will." Death will be dealt with in the section entitled "Transitoriness"; and absurdity and isolation will be dealt with in the section entitled "Meaning."

3. Here man is viewed as a mere mechanism, and in order to properly examine a mechanism it must be dismantled to its component parts and see precisely how they interact with each other. This reductionism is the "two fold notion that larger things can be shown to be merely clusters of smaller things assembled according to the standard physical laws or that the behavior of complex beings can be shown to be the law-like outcome of the behavior of less complex entities acting in concert." Niall McLaren, "Kandel's "New Science of Mind" for Psychiatry and the limits of reductionism: A critical review," *Ethical Human Psychology and Psychiatry*, 10, 2, (2008), 109.

4. Neil Wollman "*Jung and Freud compared on two types of reductionism*," 158. According to Wollman, 151 It is Freud's emphasis on biology that places him in the substrate reductionistic mold. Freud's biological roots evolved early in his career from his medical-biological interests and close associations with the physiologist Ernst

Brucke and the physician Wilhelm Fliess. Freud did his pre-medical studies under his mentor Brucke. Brucke, along with his friends Emil du Bois, Carl Ludwig and Herman von Helmholtz, held that "no other forces than the common physical-chemical ones are active within the organism."

5. By "counter-scientific" is meant an approach that does not believe that reductionism is the only way of understanding humanity and the mind. In taking this different approach Frankl is following the Kantian view that "we can understand the various parts of anything in relation to how we view the whole." Wollman, 149.

6. It is best to understand Frankl's push toward a unified dimensionalism in relation to a number of other psychotherapeutic trends that were predominant at the time of his early career. It is always difficult to determine what can be considered an influence on Frankl versus a theory that simply shares commonalities with Frankl's anthropology. As such, it is best to view the following approaches as theories that Frankl appears to have viewed in a positive light, feeling free to draw from their wells of ideas in order to formulate his own unique existential understanding of man. In terms of Frankl's general thrust against reductionism, the three primary approaches that share commonalities with him are Gestalt therapy, Phenomenology, and Adlerian Individual Psychology.

The most obvious place to start is with the meaning of the term "Gestalt." This term actually is a German reference to a complete intact whole, and therefore summarizes the essential thrust of this approach; that the client cannot be separated into parts (psychic drives, etc.) without losing the essence of the person. Based upon this idea, Gestalt therapy is interested in the whole person, and holism takes priority over any particular area of the person's life. Within this general framework, the therapist is able attend to the client's behaviors, embodiment, memories, dreams, thoughts, and feelings. This is considered the "figure" of the therapy session, characterized by those components of the individual that are considered salient at that particular moment of therapy. In conjunction with this, the "ground" refers to those aspects that are presently outside of the client's awareness, or the background context that the client exists within.

In relation to general Gestalt theory, it is clear that Frankl's stance against reductionism parallels the Gestalt push to consider the whole within therapy. Furthermore, Frankl makes the point that it provides a context for understanding the dimensionalism of man, and he makes an effort to highlight that this is central to Logotherapy. However, Frankl is not strictly Gestalt, as he wishes to clarify that while Gestalt psychotherapy has some valuable ideas, he simply uses these ideas to clarify his own logotherapeutic position. An example of this is when Frankl clarifies the experience of meaning, on page 38 of his book, *The Unheard Cry for Meaning*, "for in Gestalt perception in the traditional sense of the term we are perceiving a figure against a background; in finding meaning however, we are perceiving a possibility embedded in reality."

Another general theme of Gestalt therapy that is similar to Frankl's approach is the principle of "Phenomenological Inquiry" based upon the idea that client's must discover power in the here and now. According to Gestalt theory, a common problem that client's present is despairing over mistakes or ruminating on missed opportunities or the grieving over lost possible futures. That as a client focuses attention on what was or live in a fantastical future, that their power of choice in the present is diminished. As such, the method of phenomenological inquiry, by asking questions such as "what" and "how" are often more beneficial than asking "why" questions. This promotes awareness of the moment, for example, by asking "What is your experience right now" allows the client to experience the present and detach themselves from the feelings of the past or future. This then clarifies the client's present thinking by detaching them from their feelings, allowing a safer exploration of the client's feelings related to emotionally laden concerns.

In general this idea of phenomenological inquiry derives from the works of the late nineteenth-century philosopher Franz Brentano and early twentieth-century mathematician/phenomenologist Edmund Husserl, who wished to emphasize the need to understand people in their concrete lived experience. Early in Husserl's writings, he emphasized a transcendental position where it was important to bracket off one's attitudes and stand outside of lived experience in order to reveal the world as it was. This was later revised by the concept of the "lifeworld," where we recognize that experience is important, and that meaning is given priority in our natural attitude. In order to uncover this meaning, we must engage in phenomenological reduction by examining the difference between the world as it is, and the meanings that color our subjectivity. Frankl was aware of phenomenological ideas, highlighting that Logotherapy leans heavily on phenomenological analysis. However, it seems that his ideas did not originate solely from phenomenology, as references to phenomenology proper only appear near the end of his career. Frankl mentions that Logotherapy employs phenomenological analysis and phenomenological ideas in *Man's Search for Ultimate Meaning*, 122–128. In addition, while he does employ phenomenological ideas he only makes one passing reference to the key phenomenological theorists. Frankl is clear that a phenomenological analysis of the man in the street reveals that they cannot be understood in merely reductionistic terms.

The final theory related to Frankl's reaction to reductionism was that of Adler, for even today Frankl is recognized as a "friend" of Adler in terms of his affinity to Adlerian Individual Psychology. Although Frankl broke with Adler because he was too reductionistic, nevertheless, Adlerian psychology is well recognized as an approach that was less reductionistic than Freud's; it emphasized that people were motivated by more than sexual urges. Adlerianism also recognizes that behavior is purposeful and goal-directed, emphasizing choice and responsibility within the life of the client. As such, it seems clear that Frankl could not help but be influenced by his old mentor in formulating his views about the nature of humanity and the need to think in terms of a unified dimensionalism.

7. Frankl, *The Unheard Cry for Meaning*, 17.
8. Frankl, *Unheard Cry for Meaning,* 19.
9. Frankl, *Psychotherapy and Existentialism*, 137.
10. Frankl, *The Unheard Cry for Meaning*, 47.
11. Ibid.
12. In infinite regress in a series of propositions arises if the truth of proposition 1 requires the support of proposition 2, the truth of proposition 2 requires the support of proposition 3 and so on into infinity.

13. Frankl, *The Unheard Cry for Meaning*, 48.
14. Ibid., 49.
15. Frankl, *Psychotherapy and Existentialism*, 137.
16. Frankl, *Will to Meaning*, 17.
17. When Logotherapy included the noological dimension in psychology it meant in particular the noetic or spiritual, while trying to avoid association with formal religion. While psychoanalysis considers only the instinctual unconscious, Frankl pointed out the existence of the "spiritual" (noetic) unconscious. It is the realm of the conscience, art and love, it manifests itself in responsibleness, moral conscience, intuition, and artistic creativity, for example. When comparing Frankl and Scheler, Agnes Ponsaran writes, "Frankl agrees with Scheler that where man's heart is attached, there for him is the core of essences of things. Frankl added the dimension of meaning justifying that "only the search for meaning can lead to a life where the heart can come to terms with the past, live responsibly in the present, and plan with realistic optimism for the future." Frankl and Scheler begin the task of awakening oneself as the bearer of values. Both of them recognized conscience as the centerpiece of the noetic dimension. Whereas conscience may speak to us we have the freedom to respond yes or no to its promptings. They also share the belief that the human dimension enables us to go beyond ourselves. The fact of transcendence is stressed by both thinkers." Agnes Ponsaran, "The Philosophical Foundations of Viktor Frankl's Logotherapy." *Phillipiniana Sacra*, 42, no. 125, (2007), 351.
18. Ibid., 18.
19. Frankl, *The Doctor and the Soul*, 145–146.
20. Frankl's interest in the existential experience of the man in the street and the fully human experience of love seems to correspond with Martin Heidegger's view of Care, as he states in section 183, p. 227 of *Being and Time*, "Dasein's Being reveals itself in *care*. . . . Accordingly our existential Interpretation of Dasein as care requires pre-ontological confirmation. This lies in demonstrating that no sooner has Dasein expressed anything about itself to itself, than it has already interpreted itself as care, even though it has done so only pre-ontologically." Elsewhere in *Being and Time* (Section 119, p. 155), Heidegger examines the nature of Being and the role of placement, this is something that Frankl clearly picks up on. The term that Heidegger used to sum up his key points of context and Being is "Dasein" (roughly translated as Being-in-the-World). This phrase pointed not to a reductionistic view of Being, but to the role of the whole in forming and experiencing meaning. There are meanings interwoven within meanings within Being, and they are inseparable from Being itself. Being-in-the-World is a structure which is primordially and constantly whole . . . this structure has been elucidated phenomenally as a whole, and also in its constitutive items Dasein exists factically. Because Dasein essentially has a state-of-mind belonging to it, Dasein has a kind of Being in which it is brought before itself and becomes disclosed to itself in its thrownness.

According to Heidegger's *Being and Time*, Dasein's "average everydayness" can be defined as Being-in-the-world which is falling and disclosed, thrown and projected, and for which its own most potentiality-for-Being is an issue, both in its Being alongside the "world" and in its "Being-with" Others/Mit-sein. According to Heidegger in *Being and Time* (Sections 193–194, pp 237–238) "The formally existential totality of Dasein's ontological structural whole must therefore be grasped in the following structure: the Being of Dasein means ahead-of-itself-Being-already-in-(the world) as Being-alongside (entities encountered within-the-world). The Being fills in the signification of the term "care" [Sorge], which is used in a purely ontologico-existential manner. From this signification every tendency of Being which one might have in mind ontically, such as worry [Besorgnis] or carefreeness [Sorglosigkeit], is ruled out. The phenomenon of care in its totality is essentially something that cannot be torn asunder; so any attempts to trace it back to special acts or drives like willing and wishing or urge and addiction, or to construct it out of these, will be unsuccessful." These ideas of Heidegger clearly fit well with Frankl's first principle of his anthropology: Unified Dimensionism.

These basic steps of the phenomenological interpretation of being are then picked up by Frankl, along with the overall importance of care. The therapeutic dialogue helps the client to reach a standing in the world (in line with Heidegger's Dasein). There is a subtle difference between Heidegger and Frankl, however; that is, Frankl believed that meaning (logos) lived out in service is the most primitive and powerful part of Being-in-the-World, whereas Heidegger viewed understanding as the key. Frankl picked up on this idea within his work, *The Unheard Cry for Meaning* on 46–47, and pointed out that a key to it is self-transcendence: "Something analogous holds for man. He too is sometimes portrayed as if he were merely a closed system within which cause-effect relations, such as conditioned or unconditioned reflexes, are operant." On the other hand, being human is profoundly characterized as being open to the world, as Max Scheler, Arnold Gehlen and Adolf Portmann have shown. Or, as Martin Heidegger said, being human is "Being-in-the-World." According to Frankl what is called the self-transcendence of existence denotes the fundamental fact that being human means relating to something, or someone, other than oneself. And existence falters and collapses unless this self-transcendent quality is lived out.

It is clear that meaning is important to Frankl; however, to simply say that logos is the key to existence for Frankl is to make an artificial separation between Frankl and Heidegger. For there is a place where both seem to draw a real world connection with human existence and meaning, and that is to be found in what Heidegger calls "Care" and Frankl calls "Love." Heidegger expresses it in *Being and Time* (section 231) this way, "In Being-in-the-World, whose essential structures centre in disclosedness, we have found the basic state of the entity we have taken on our theme. The totality of Being-in-the-World as a structural whole has revealed itself in **Care**. In Care the Being of Dasein is included." Though thick with his philosophical speak, Heidegger does recognize that Care envelopes this Being-in-the-World. Frankl also esteems this Care, but uses the more common term of "love" to draw out its meaning in the human experience.

21. Frankl, *The Doctor and the Soul,* 134.
22 Ibid., 132.
23. Frankl, *The Doctor and the Soul,* 132–133.
24. Ibid., 147.
25. Ibid.
26. Frankl, *The Unconscious God: Psychotherapy and Theology*, 84–85.

27. A footnote within Frankl, *The Doctor and the Soul*, 93.

28. According to Jean-Paul Sartre *Being and Nothingness* (New York: Washington Square, 1992), 62–63: In explaining how I apprehend the absence of Pierre in the room, it would be useless to invoke those famous "empty intentions" of Husserl, which are in great part constitutive of perception. . . . To be empty an intention must be conscious of itself as empty and precisely as empty of the exact matter which it aims. An empty intention constitutes itself as empty to the extent that it posits its matter as nonexisting or absent. In short, an empty intention is a consciousness of negation which transcends itself toward an object which it posits as absent or nonexistent.

Thus whatever may be the explanation which we give it, Pierre's absence, in order to be established or realized, requires a negative moment by which consciousness, in the absence of all prior determination, constitutes itself as negation. If in terms of my perceptions of the room, I conceive of the former inhabitant who is no longer in the room, I am of necessity forced to produce an act of thought which no prior state can determine nor motivate, in short to effect in myself a break with being. And in so far as I continually use negatites to isolate and determine existents – that is, to think them – the succession of my "states of consciousness" is a perpetual separation of effect from cause, since every nihilating process must derive its source only from itself. Inasmuch as my present state which be prolongation of my prior state, every opening by which negation could slip through would be completely blocked. Every psychic process of nihilation implies then a cleavage between the immediate psychic past and the present. This cleavage is precisely nothingness. At least, someone will say, there remains the possibility of successive implication between the nihilating process.

29. According to Sartre, *Being and Nothingness*, 679–680:

The bourgeois makes himself a bourgeois by denying that there are any classes, just as the worker makes himself a worker by asserting that classes exist and by realizing through his revolutionary activity his "being-in-a-class." But these external limits of freedom, precisely because they are external and are interiorized only as unrealizables, will never be either a real obstacle for freedom or a limit suffered. Freedom is total and infinite, which does not mean that it has no limits but that it never encounters them. The only limits which freedom bumps up against at each moment are those which it imposes on itself and of which we have spoken in connection with the past, with the environment, and with techniques.

30. Jean Paul Sartre, *Being and Nothingness* (New York, NY: Washington Square Press, 1992), 2–189.

31. Frankl, *Man's Search for Meaning*, 86.

32. According to Sartre, *Being and Nothingness,* 711, the nature of freedom defines a person, as it is itself the ground of a person's meaning:

Under these conditions since every event in the world can be revealed to me only as an opportunity (an opportunity made use of, lacked, neglected, etc.), or better yet since everything which happens to us can be considered as a chance (i.e., can appear to us only as a way of realizing this being which is in question in our being) and since others as transcendences-transcended are themselves only opportunities and chances, the responsibility of the for-itself extends to the entire world as a peopled-world. It is precisely thus that the for-itself apprehends itself in anguish; that is, as a being which is neither the foundation of its own being nor of the Other's being nor of the in-itself which form the world, but a being which is compelled to decide the meaning of being – within it and everywhere outside of it. The one who realizes in anguish his conditions as being thrown into a responsibility which extends to his very abandonment has no longer either remorse or regret or excuse; he is no longer anything but a freedom which perfectly reveals itself and whose being resides in this very revelation. But as we point out at the beginning of this work, most of the time we flee anguish in bad faith.

33. Sartre, *Being and Nothingness,* 80–84.

34. Frankl, *Psychotherapy and Existentialism*, 12.

35. Sartre, *Being and Nothingness*, 303–419.

36. T. Z. Lavine, *From Socrates to Sartre* (New York, NY: Bantam Books), 349.

37. Lavine, *From Socrates to Sartre,* 351–363.

38. Sartre, *Being and Nothingness,* 191–347.

39. Frankl, *Man's Search for Ultimate Meaning*, 64.

40. Jean Paul Sartre, *Existentialism is a Humanism* (New Haven, CT: Yale University Press, 2007), 36.

41. Frankl, *Psychotherapy and Existentialism*, 26–27.

42. Ibid., 124.

43. Part of recognizing the nature of a meaningful human life is recognizing the nature of subjective truth and the reality that we all must appreciate our own perspective in relation to the wider reality of existence. As Frankl says in *The Will to Meaning*, pages 59-60, "The . . . thing which is subjective is the perspective through which we approach reality, and this subjectiveness does not in the least detract from the objectiveness of reality itself . . . if you look through a telescope you can see something which is outside the telescope itself. And if you look at the world, or a think in the world, you also see more than, say, the perspective. What is seen through the perspective, however subjective the perspective may be, is the objective world. In fact, "seen through" is the literal meaning of the Latin word, "perspectum."

44. Frankl considers the wrestling with this question of the meaning of life to be a human achievement, rather than a neurosis.

45. Frankl's dimensional ontology gives primacy to the spiritual plane over the physical and the psychological dimensions. By incorporating them into this noetic plane he is able to bring together a unity of the whole, rather than the reduction to simple parts. Agnes Ponsaran, *The Philosophical Foundations of Viktor Frankl's Logotherapy*, 354.

46. Frankl, *Man's Search for Ultimate Meaning*, 143.

47. Frankl, *Man's Search for Meaning,* 82.

48. Frankl, *Man's Search for Ultimate Meaning*, 142.

49. Noodynamics is the balance of tension within the temporality of man, between what man is and what man strives to be and the meanings to fulfill. It is generally agreed among existentialists that future tense is more unique in defining the human condition. For example, Martin Heidegger claimed that "the primary meaning of existentiality is the future." When discussing time, he "always mentioned the future first . . . to indicate that the future has a priority in . . . authentic temporality." As members

of the animal world, we are motivated by survival and we function accordingly. Being conscious of future time, however, allows us to give meaning to our existence so that we construct purposes for survival that create future goals. Being self-transcendent, we decide whether life is meaningful or meaningless. To fully comprehend human beings is impossible without understand what purposes pull us into the future and what meanings we attach to these purposes. Andrew Lester, *Hope in Pastoral Care and Counseling* (Louisville, KY: Westminster John Knox Press, 1995), 17.

50. Frankl, *Psychotherapy and Existentialism*, 83.

51. Frankl, *Psychotherapy and Existentialism*, 56.

52. Ibid., 41.

53. Frankl argues that the transitory aspects of life are the potentialities that are rescued in present action and become irrevocably stored in the past.

54. Frankl asserts that transitoriness of life only really applies to the possibilities of life; once these possibilities for meaning are actualized, they are secure and provide the ground for a meaningful life.

55. Frankl, *Psychotherapy and Existentialism,* 128.

Chapter 5

Legacy

Living a long and productive 92 years, Viktor Frankl spent each day in learning, teaching, and loving. He learned to struggle with the most difficult problems of existence. Teaching existential truths in simple language. Living out the meaning of love in his actions. Living a life of service to his family, his patients, his profession, and his intellectual child, Logotherapy.[1]

In looking at the life of eminent people, their lives often fit within a particular creative mold.[2] As we can see from his childhood through to his old age, dogged hard work and perseverance were part of developing Frankl's theories, and later his worldwide fame.[3] If one considers the lives of individuals who transform disciplines, they are typically people who have unanswered questions; with Frankl, the question grew out of his childhood intuition. During his childhood he knew implicitly from his parents, and directly from the religious parts of his education, that meaning permeates human existence. Then, in his teenage years, his ideas were emerging into a coherent understanding. While he did not have all the answers, young Viktor's intense objection to his science teacher's statement that "life is nothing but combustion" shows that he knew there was meaning beyond reductionism. He set himself to the task of discovering the meanings inherent within life.

Yet many people seek out meanings within life, but do not change their field of study. For while struggling with the issues of meaning implicitly and explicitly, he drew upon insights from psychiatry and neurology. Moreover, he became an existential philosopher.

Researchers say that in changing a discipline, a person starts with an interest, curiosity, and drive. The person internalizes the system and thinks in innovative ways.[4] Once the person learns to take seriously the rules, problems, and conflicts within this system, he is able to work to engage these problems. It is clear that early in his professional life, Frankl commits to changing his domain, applying to Freud's Society and becoming a supporter of Adler. This allows him to become aware of what others are doing in the field, while clarifying his own position within the discipline. In addition, the freedom Frankl experiences in his clinical supervision allows him to begin to flesh out some of his ideas of meaning, and its importance within therapy. This is all part of the process that forms and molds Frankl into the creative thinker that set his sights on dramatically influencing psychotherapy.[5]

Frankl commits himself to engaging the intellectual community, succeeding as a therapist and neurologist, and connecting with the man in the street. He spends time in his medical profession, and also enjoys leisurely pursuits with friends, like his mountain-climbing excursions. All of this nurtures a flexible personality able to meet the needs of any situation. In addition, his experiences just before, and within the concentration camps, hone his skills to take complex ideas and bring them to the everyday level. It is as if he wrestles the deep meanings of heaven, and pulls them down into the camp meetings, to provide comfort to suffering people. This intellectual and personal flexibility is crucial to Frankl's success. He uses the ideas of the man in the street as the plumb line of any deep philosophical ideas about therapy.[6]

To change a field or discipline an individual typically needs to develop an interest at an early age. Second, the individual needs to be able to engage the field; third, the person needs to have the flexibility to engage various contexts. It is clear that Frankl's early life set him up to be an influence. Psychological researchers also highlight that once approximately 10,000 hours are set to the idea or problem, that the person makes major contributions.[7] We see this level of dedication very early within Frankl's professional life. He clearly put in the effort to better understand the role of meaning in life. After years of dedication to the task of clarifying meaning in life, the principles became clear. Crossing this hurdle, Frankl was finally able to write his first work, outlining the principles of Logotherapy.

Psychological researchers also suggest the quality and quantity of work is greater at the beginning of one's career, and then gradually tapers off. In some cases however, there is a swan song, a work near the end of the individual's professional life that rivals those at the beginning. This is something we see with Viktor Frankl's life. His early works, *The Doctor and the Soul* and *Man's Search for Meaning*, were extremely creative and popular. *The Doctor and the Soul* outlines the essentials of Logotherapy. *Man's Search for Meaning* sells millions of copies while connecting Logotherapy to his own survival story in the concentration camps. In a sense, all of Frankl's later works were elaborations on these two books. Of course, Frankl still works tirelessly to meet the continual need to sell his ideas, in order to bring about lasting change. We see this effort in Frankl's book *A Will to Meaning*, as the concluding chapter passes the leadership of Logotherapy on to the next generation.

LATER LIFE

Upon retiring from his position as chief of neurology in 1970, Frankl's travel and lecture schedule became even more intense. Lecturing at more than 200 universities, not including those within Europe. His favorite was the United States International University (USIU) in San Diego, California. In the period from 1970 to 1990, Frankl returns to lecture here and to spend time with the prominent father of client-centered therapy, Carl Rogers. Frankl even takes a year to serve as the distinguished professor of Logotherapy at USIU.[8]

Despite this academic posting, Frankl did experience challenges within the culture of his long-term posting at the University of Vienna; and specifically within the neurological-psychiatric establishment. As such, Frankl was promoted to the level of associate professor, but never full professor. Ironically, the two men who were also founders of Vienna psychological schools and greatly admired by Frankl, Freud and Adler, also failed to achieve the position of full professor.[9]

After 40 years traveling the globe to promote his life's passion, Logotherapy, he was starting to slow down by the 1990s. Audiences loved his personal charisma, and his message. Known as the human dynamo that sparks U.S. colleges, he loved the lecture circuit.[10] His second wife Eleonore, "Elly," often accompanying his lecture tours, including four around the world tours. At the age of 91, Frankl finally stops touring. This was a difficult decision, and came only after cancelling a number of tours due to poor health. This was especially frustrating as his mind was getting better with old age, and he was better able to express the essence of Logotherapy.

At the end of his career Frankl gives a swan song, as he builds upon the title of his most popular book *Man's Search for Meaning*, capitalizing upon the central implicit tenet of his earliest work, *The Doctor and the Soul*. With *Man's Search for Ultimate Meaning*, a reworking of previous books, Frankl engages the central theme of freedom that is so crucial for existential psychotherapy. He then adds the importance of ultimate concern and responsibility as a capstone to his life's work.

CULMINATING THEORIES

In the later years of his life Frankl recaptures his life's work and summarizes it within the context of ultimate meaning. His goal is to move existential psychotherapy past freedom to responsibility. It is, in essence, a call to consider the importance of spirituality within psychotherapy. This unifying theme summarizes *Man's Search for Ultimate Meaning*. The reverberations of this theme forming part of Frankl's legacy.

Frankl's life and work reach a pinnacle as he turns his full attention to ultimate meaning. It is here that he clarifies the tension between the human lived-world and higher meanings. In *Man's Search for Ultimate Meaning*, Frankl remains with his tried and true philosophy. He provides an exploration of human existence that encompasses both psychology and religion. He points out that the relationship between psychology and spirituality is important, as it exists within people. We cannot truly understand or appreciate someone's humanness until we recognize them as spiritual beings.[11]

BEING FULLY HUMAN

Spirituality

One important feature of Frankl's contribution, so obvious that it should not need mentioning, is often overlooked: his call to remember the humanness of the client.[12] Frankl makes it clear that psychiatry and religion are disciplines that encompass different dimensions of the same reality. He points out that higher dimensions of reality may subsume the lower within them.[13]

Respecting and being fully human is the whole goal of Logotherapy. The goal is to understand ourselves as a whole being, constantly emerging, exercising both freedom and responsibility.[14] As a psychotherapeutic practice, Logotherapy concerns itself with helping a person to recognize the power to choose, and the responsibility in choosing. Responsibility emerges within the higher dimension of theology. For it is only from the spiritual perspective that responsibility makes full sense.[15] Spirituality, freedom, and responsibility are core to Frankl's sense of being human. It is the hub of whom he is as a person. He treasures his spiritual traditions, and in his maturity actively reconnects with his early experiences of spirituality.[16]

Self-Transcendence

Self-transcendence is fundamental to Logotherapy, and the meaning of humanness. In his old age Frankl continues his work despite ever increasing physical trials. Nearing the end of his life, the work goes on despite being almost blind, with only indistinct images remaining in one eye. His wife Elly assumes a greater portion of the load. She reads everything to him, challenging her own abilities to keep pace.[17]

Freedom to Be Responsible

Frankl believes that people are supremely self-determining. He recognized the limits imposed by biology, social, and other influences, but believes people are free to take a stand, even against these limits. People have a choice. Frankl witnessed many examples in the concentration camps that he called a *living laboratory* and a *testing ground.*[18] He and his fellow prisoners, "watched and witnessed some of our comrades behave like swine while others behaved like saints. Man has both potentialities within himself; which one is actualized depends on decisions but not on conditions."[19]

In Frankl's view, people have freedom, but not only freedom. People also have responsibility as a counterbalance to freedom. Responsibility implies a sense of duty for something or to someone. Responsibility creates a connection between people and the world: the people, the things, and the opportunities. If people use their freedom to act responsibly in the world, then each person likely finds meaning in life. The individual finds meaning outside the self. The outward journey is where meaning reveals itself. People must be self-transcendent to find meaning. Frankl recognizes that humanity does not always want to accept responsibility for decision making. He says that there is something deep and mysterious about responsibility that resembles an abyss. It causes a person to shudder because "there is something fearful about man's responsibility. But at the same time something glorious!"[20, 21]

The Voice of Conscience

In *Man's Search for Ultimate Meaning*, Frankl teaches that Logotherapy is the psychotherapeutic method of helping a person to recognize the self. We then come back to religion and spirituality. In spirituality we understand the human need for responsibility. We aren't aware of entire mind, but the voice of conscience is always there, emerging into consciousness when we ignore responsibility.

Our existence resides within freedom, the realm of possibilities. However, what limits freedom, facticity, is also present. Here the spiritual struggle exists, between our facticity and our existential freedom exercised in possibility. People labor in the *in-between* tension, for spirituality brings wholeness to a person.[22] Spirituality is a thing-in-itself; it is whole and irreducible.[23] It is within this wholeness that Frankl sees the conscience to emerge. Though this conscience is largely unconscious, we ignore it at our existential peril. Frankl believes the voice of conscience is always there. However, people may anesthetize themselves *against* the voice of their own conscience.[24] For Frankl, it is essential that the voice of conscience be always present. Meaning emerges whenever following the guidance of conscience in action. For Frankl, being conscientious implies self-transcendence and the ability to view our own moral choices.[25]

The conscience is spiritual, experienced as both unconscious and conscious. For consciousness only makes sense as a summative experience of thought. Something that emerges from the unconscious for an examination of the self. In this view, consciousness is a small part of the unconscious. Frankl quotes *Vedic literature* in summarizing this idea: "That which does the seeing, cannot be seen; that which does the hearing, cannot be heard; and that which does the thinking, cannot be thought."[26] The conscience then is something other than the conscious self.[27] There is a transcendent quality to the voice of conscience. So it is not simply an unconscious product that springs into consciousness. Conscience connects us to the transcendent, reminding us we are responsible to God.

Genuine Religion

Conscience is an expression of our humanness, seizing the spiritual disposition of the unconscious. We have conscience, and love is the personal expression of conscience, in responsibility. Conscience is a means for understanding one's spiritual core.[28] G*enuine religion* is existential, where a person commits in deliberate choosing. In Logotherapy then, the therapist and patient can explore the religious life, as part of the patient's existential authenticity.[29]

THE END OF LIFE

At the age of 90, Viktor was suffering from chest pains and shortness of breath.[30] While his mind was getting better with age, his body was wearing out. In 1996, Frankl's sister Stella died, and the news was a serious blow to Frankl and his health.[31] By mid-1997, Frankl was doing poorly and his heart was giving out. Frankl made the decision to undergo bypass surgery, knowing that he might not survive. He survived the surgery, but never regained consciousness. Three days after surgery, Nazi camp Prisoner #119,104 died in Vienna on September 2, 1997.

> In keeping with Jewish tradition, Viktor was buried immediately after his death. The family was offered a place of honor where Viktor could be buried in Vienna's Central Cemetery. But Viktor had already chosen to be buried in the family plot in the old Jewish part of the cemetery. In the words of Alexander, "He wanted to be buried the way he was born, somebody not known to the world, in a very simple way." Viktor's grave is beneath the headstone where his maternal grandmother is buried. The names of his parents, Elsa and Gabriel, and his brother and sister-in-law, Walter and Else Frankl, have been added to the headstone in memory of those who perished in the Holocaust. Beneath that are the words VIKTOR EMIL FRANKL, 26. MARCH 1905–2. SEPTEMBER 1997. Nothing is written there about all his accomplishments and awards. And yet there is a silent reminder of the many lives Viktor Frankl touched: The marker is

> covered with smooth round pebbles. By Jewish custom, small stones are placed at the gravesite by those who wish to honor the person who died.[32]

Frankl's death was made public but was hardly noticed because of its timing. Only two days earlier, Princess Diana was killed in a tragic car accident in Paris. The world's media followed every detail of her death and funeral preparations. Then, just three days after Frankl's death, Mother Teresa died at the age of 87 in Calcutta (now Kolkata). Sandwiching Frankl's death between the deaths of two world-famous women. Consequently, his passing didn't receive the notice that it might have.

With Viktor Frankl now gone, we are left with only his legacy. That legacy is a call to rehumanize psychotherapy. To know that meaning in life is waiting to reveal itself through the actions we do. Meaning exists on many levels, from the ultimate meanings that are, in many ways, ungraspable, to the small personal meanings that fill everyone's lives. Viktor Frankl is dead, but the meaning of his work remains. His legacy continues to touch people's lives. Even the smallest and most personal of meanings can be powerful, as we see in an experience of his widow Elly:

> After Viktor was gone, Elly searched the apartment for the hidden book he had told her about. Finally one day when she was dusting the books in his study, she found . . . *Suffering Man,* which seemed to have slipped behind the others. Elly pulled it forward and opened it. When the book was published, Viktor had dedicated it to Elly with one word: *Elly*. Now Elly saw that above her printed name, Viktor had written the word *For*. Below it, he had written more words, so that the entire page read: *For Elly, Who succeeded in changing a suffering man into a loving man. Viktor.*[33]

Frankl lived a life that was dedicated to the fullness of humanity. His allegiance to Logotherapy sprouted out of a desire to better serve his patients, and grew into something greater. Frankl's influence and creative thought now live on in his works, and in the lives of those he influenced. The final pages will explore how the field of psychotherapy continues to be influenced by the ideas and directions advocated by Frankl.

CRITICS AND FRIENDS

Frankl was a man who sought to live a life of self-transcendence. In many ways he succeeded, creating a legacy that extends into many areas of research and practice within psychology. Within this chapter, we will explore the legacy of Frankl, those that criticized him, as well as those who followed along the same philosophical path.

YALOM AS CRITIC

Irvin Yalom, in his book *Existential Psychotherapy* gave comprehensive coverage to the four pillars of existential thought: death, freedom, isolation, and meaninglessness. In the section on meaninglessness, Yalom mentioned Frankl many times, acknowledging him as one of the few clinicians to make a substantial contribution to the role of meaning in psychotherapy. Yalom also gave Frankl credit for maintaining a consistent, focused interest on meaning throughout his career. In Yalom's opinion, Frankl made an important contribution by taking the issue of meaning out of the realm of philosophical abstraction and placing it squarely in front of the therapist. Yet, for all his praise of Frankl, Yalom found plenty in Frankl's work to criticize.[34]

Yalom wrote about Frankl's style and method: "His arguments are often appeals to emotion; he persuades, makes *ex cathedra* proclamations, and is often repetitive and strident."[35] Yalom claimed that many scholars found Frankl's method "offensive"[36]: "Frankl's position is basically religious and rests on the assumption that there is a God who has ordained a meaning for each of us to discover and fulfill."[37]

Yalom also objected to Frankl's theory which maintained that meaning is *out there* in the world, waiting to be discovered by each person. Man cannot invent it but must discover it. Yalom explained his criticism this way:

> An existential position holds that the world is contingent – that is, everything that is could as well have been otherwise; that human beings constitute themselves, their world, and their situation within that world; that there exists no "meaning," no grand design in the universe, no guidelines for living other than those the individual creates.[38]

Yalom admitted that man likes to have meaning, even that: "we crave meaning and are uncomfortable in its absence."[39] But what was the source of that meaning? Did it come from inside man or from outside? If from inside, as the traditional existentialists believed, then there was a menacing follow-up question: "How does a being who needs meaning find meaning in a universe that has no meaning?"[40] If from outside, as Frankl firmly believed, then there was the implication of divine orderliness, suggesting a God. Yalom took issue with the God argument, saying: "After all, if there were a God, why should it follow that He had a purpose for life. . . . The belief that life is incomplete without goal fulfillment is not so much a tragic existential fact of life as it is a Western myth, a cultural artifact."[41]

For Frankl, one of the ways to find meaning in life was by creating a work or doing a deed. This path to achievement and success through work, Frankl thought was a path to experience meaning that most people should find obvious. Finding it not so obvious, Yalom disagreed with Frankl on this point. Yalom argued by looking at other cultures, especially Eastern cultures, which have a different view of life based upon a fundamentally different attitude toward nature. He explained it this way:

> The Westerner is analytical and objective and attempts to understand nature by dissecting and then subjugating and exploiting it. The Oriental is subjective, integrative, totalizing, and he attempts not to analyze and harness nature but to experience and harmonize with it. The contrast, then, is between a searching action mode and a harmonizing-union one, and often is phrased in terms of "doing" versus "being."[42]

Yalom argued that all people were not "do-ers," as Frankl's theory would suggest, and becoming a "do-er" or a "be-er" depended on where one lived and how one was acculturated.

Near the end of his life Klingberg had a discussion with Frankl about the controversies and criticisms encountered over the years. Frankl seemed content to have endured the comments of all dissenters when he shared the following:

> Would it be better to try to please everyone and say nothing important and worthwhile? Should I keep silent about my deepest convictions just to acquire some shallow approval? And what is most important after all, appearance or substance? Look at the mail, which nobody knows about: for every reproach hundreds of thank-you notes from people who are nobody in the eyes of the world. This is what is important, that people find meaning in their lives no matter what the world throws at them. It really doesn't matter a damn that a few people have called me this or that or have said one thing or another against me – even one letter from someone who has overcome despair cancels all of that.[43]

Despite all of these criticisms, Yalom still acknowledges that Viktor Frankl's contribution to the field was invaluable and in many ways under-appreciated:

> He has, in my opinion, made an important contribution to psychotherapy theory, he has not gained the recognition he deserves from the academic community.
>
> In part this neglect may be a function of the content of Frankl's thought which, like most contributions to existential therapy, can find no home in the "better" academic neighborhoods. Logotherapy belongs neither to psychoanalytically oriented schools, nor to formal psychiatry, nor to religious studies, nor to behaviorally oriented academic psychology, nor even to the "pop" personal growth movement . . . . Furthermore, many scholars find Frankl's method offensive. . . . Still, I would urge the reader to persevere. Frankl has made a significant contribution in placing the issue of meaning before the therapist and in his many penetrating insights into the clinical implications of the search for meaning.[44]

Even through his criticisms, Yalom admits that Frankl has done much to further the role of meaning within human experience. Frankl's influence has been both direct and indirect; in the following pages, we will discuss those who may be considered "friends" of Frankl and those who are ardent "torchbearers."

FRIENDS OF FRANKL

There are many prominent psychotherapists who were influenced by Frankl to a greater or lesser degree. While some may not be considered strong disciples of Frankl, they do drink from the same intellectual well of existentialism. In light of Frankl's vast impact upon the field of existential psychotherapy, it is imperative that a number of these leaders be mentioned.

Boss and Binswanger

Two contemporaries of Frankl were Medard Boss and Ludwig Binswanger, proponents of an existentially based psychotherapeutic approach known as *Daseinsanalysis*. Frankl himself drew a parallel with Binswanger's, while pointing out a divergent starting point: "Binwanger's work boils down to an application of Heideggerian concepts to psychiatry. . . . Logotherapy is the result of an application of Max Scheler's concepts to psychotherapy."[45]

Like Logotherapy, Daseinsanalysis was an attempt to construe a more dignified and holistic understanding of human existence. It was a reaction to Freud's attempts to understand human beings as a reductionistic collection of causal mechanisms, drives, and instincts. Its first proponent, Ludwig Binswanger, sought to develop in the 1930s a phenomenological anthropology based on Heidegger's idea of being human, "Being-in-the-World." However, his critique of some of Heidegger's ideas may have led to his later diminished role in the movement.[46]

It was Medard Boss, who in the 1950s befriended Heidegger and really popularized the ideals of Daseinsanalysis. The first key ingredient in the Boss' and Heidegger branch of Daseinsanalysis was therapy set within the context of being. That is, human beings are attached to the environment within which they exist, and they must be considered as fundamentally connected. The second aspect of Boss's thought was that the human experience is one of the world disclosing openness, providing possibilities to be actualized. The final key concept was that human beings cannot be reduced to a theoretical superstructure of psychic apparatus and conflicting intrapsychic Freudian dynamics.[47]

Like Frankl, Boss was against the reductionism of Freudian psychoanalysis. Like Frankl, Boss was interested in creating a more humanizing therapy based upon existential principles. Like Frankl, Boss was steeped in traditional analytic practice and was comfortable with a therapist-led approach, including such practices as having the client lie on the couch, or encouraging "free association." One difference between Frankl and Boss is that Boss rejected the notion of the unconscious. In contrast, Frankl finds value in the concept of the unconscious. Frankl preferred to reject the dehumanizing trend of Freudian psychodynamics as an all-encompassing system, rather than reject this fundamental part of the human mind. So despite a great deal of similarity, Logotherapy and Daseinsanalysis never merged and unlike Logotherapy, Daseinsanalysis failed to gain a strong foothold in the English-speaking world.

Erwin Straus and Eugene Minkowski

Erwin Straus was in many ways a man with similar passions to Frankl. Born into the family of a wealthy German banker, Straus studied both medicine and philosophy. He was profoundly influenced by the work of Carl Jung as well as that of Husserl and Scheler. In the 1920s Straus began to engage in the anthropological psychiatry of Binswanger, developing friendships with both Binswanger and the French psychiatrist, Eugene Minkowski. Because of his mother's Jewish heritage, Straus came under scrutiny during the Nazi regime. In order to escape, Straus and his family utilized his mother's American citizenship to immigrate to the United States in 1938.

In the United States, Straus was able to secure a teaching position in North Carolina where he taught humanistic psychology for seven years. Returning to studies he completed his American medical and psychiatric diplomas in 1946. He then took up a position as director of research and education at the Veteran's Administration Hospital in Lexington, Kentucky. For the remainder of his years, Straus engaged in the American movement of phenomenological psychology.

The work of Straus focused on the anthropological question of how a person is in the "the process of becoming" and how this may result in disturbed behavior and pathology. In his early work entitled *The Primary World of the Senses*, Straus combines embodiment ideas from Merleau-Ponty, Being-in-the-World from Heidegger, and a hierarchy of values from Scheler. His resulting view of the patient then, was a person's life as a creative engagement, rather than simply reducing the patient to behavioral mechanisms of stimulus and response.

Within this general framework there are some obvious connections with Frankl. First, the importance of actually bodily engaging the world and expressing values is central to Frankl's view of experiencing meaning. Second, Straus' insistence that life is a poetic act rather than a reducible phenomenon is also consistent with Frankl emphasis upon the noetic dimension within Logotherapy. What Straus does differently from Frankl is to focus upon a phenomenological understanding of suggestibility, whereas Frankl remained focused upon the theory and practice of Logotherapy.

Straus' criticized the prevailing concept that the suggestibility of a person was in some way a pathology of consciousness. Rather, he suggested that suggestibility is a normal and essential part of our *Being-in-the-World.* That people make connections with other people and participate in "*We-experiences*." That the everyday experience of interaction with other people includes an element of participating in the experiential lived world of the other.[48]

The value of Straus' research in this area was clear and fit well with the emerging trend toward client-centered therapy within America. Straus pointed out that when a leader of an animal herd signals some anxiety, all the animals in the heard come to participate in this anxiety. Since this phenomenon is so much more complex within people, then logically, the therapeutic relationship should take this into consideration. A therapist that expresses a "We-experience" that portrays calm openness and care will draw the client to this way of being. Just as a therapist that suddenly says, "Oh oh," will predictably draw the patient into an experience of anxiety. In line with this idea, therapeutic trust and rapport become important factors in the "we-experience" of psychotherapy.

Another kindred spirit of Frankl's was Eugene Minkowski, a French psychiatrist. He was born into a Jewish family from St. Petersburg and obtained his medical degree in 1909 from Warsaw. He took up the study of philosophy and in 1914 finished a work entitled *The Essential Elements of Time-Quality.* During World War I, he served for the French army and after the war began to explore the lived world of his patients.

Strongly influenced by Husserl and Scheler, Minkowski employed a phenomenological approach to better understand the experience of the patient, as a person, and not just a pathology. This step toward reclaiming the humanness of the patient is clearly in line with Frankl's primary call of Logotherapy, in the rehumanizing of psychiatry as a discipline. Through the 1920s Minkowski focused his work on the experience of time as seen from the perspective of people with schizophrenia. He noted a atrophy of time experience and a loss of intuition within these individuals.

While Minkowski's work did not lead to any drastic breakthroughs in the treatment of schizophrenia, it was the first work of its kind in looking at the lived experience of the patient. This approach meant that Minkowski set the stage for a system of structural phenomenological analysis, particularly as he related it to the dimension of time.[49] This did lead to an important perspective of "becoming" when understanding the lived experience of a patient.

For Minkowski, our present life is where we transform the past into a future possibility that we identify and act toward, thus "becoming." To suffer from a psychopathology, Minkowski observed, often means a person's disconnect between the past and future. According to Minkowski, the fundamental aspect of a person's lived experience is their past-present-future connection. If that connection is disrupted or distorted, the person can develop symptoms of despondency, lack of hope, and loss of aspirations. For Minkowski then, the lived experience of psychopathology was being stuck and isolated in a disconnected present moment.

This is reflective of Frankl's idea of the noogenic neurosis, of being disconnected from the world and being overwhelmed with boredom or apathy. The counter to this, for Frankl, was to encounter meaning by exercising the layers of values. This relates to Minkowski's theory as Minkowski would see this encountering of meaning as a means of reconnecting the time experience components to enable "becoming" to exist.[50] This for Minkowski is the essential personal impetus that delivers temporal cohesiveness and is what provides a person with the hardiness to weather life's difficult times.[51]

May, Bugental, Moustakas, and Schneider

Frankl had a huge impact upon the English-speaking world with the popularity of his book *Man's Search for Meaning*. This impact, combined with his continual speaking engagements within the United States, helped raise the profile of existential influences within mental health professions. This profile was helped by a man who shares a surprising number of similarities with Frankl: Rollo May. Rollo May was born in 1909 in the United States and during his undergraduate studies spent some time in Europe where he studied with Alfred Adler. Adler's theories had a profound effect upon him, so much so that after he came back to the United States and became an ordained minister, he did not lose interest in psychology. In fact, he returned to his studies to complete his PhD in psychology from Columbia University in 1949. Like Frankl, May was also strongly influenced by the writings of Kierkegaard.

With the publication of his book *Existence: A New Dimension in Psychiatry and Psychology*, Rollo May helped to usher in an American school that has become known as an existential-humanistic approach to psychotherapy.[52] May himself was more interested in the theoretical influences of existentialism upon psychology, rather than its professional practice. He did however make a profound impact upon the American scene. He provided a good deal of insight into many aspects of life such as anxiety, life-span development, and the nature of love. Within his book *Love and Will*, he demonstrates that his basic views are similar to those of Frankl, and are drawn from the same sources, without quoting from Frankl directly. This is most notable in his discussion of the importance to be self-transcendent, or to be "out there" with our love:

> Heidegger then took the next step by removing Husserl's concept "out of the thin air" of Platonic idealism and extending it to the total feeling, valuing, acting human being. He did this by his concept of care (Sorge). Care is constitutive of our world in a sense analogous to Kant's understanding. Man is the being, Heidegger says over and over again, who is concerned about Being. And when man fails to be, we could add from our therapeutic observations of states of conformism and depersonalization, he loses his being, that is, loses his potentialities. There is a close, inner relationship between caring and intentionality, suggested already by the fact that the root word "tend" – to take care of – is the center of the term intentionality.[53]

While May wrote extensively on existential theory and became so popular he influenced other existentially informed psychologists within America: James Bugental and Clark Moustakas among the two earliest examples, and later Kirk Schneider. James Bugental was also largely influenced by the client-centered approach of Carl Rogers, and during his writing career in the 1960s through the 1990s covered most of the themes that formed the basis of Frankl's existential anthropology.

Bugental was most interested with the emotional expression and experience of meaning within life, with his first books focusing on authenticity and identity. Bugental was very interested in the emotionality of the person as an expression of the unitary expression of being. Within this principle, Bugental argued that defensive strategies that protect the individual from existential anxiety and numb some emotional discomfort, and may cause a ripple effect that can destabilize a person's entire life. Instead, each person must recognize his responsibility to make his own choices. Each person must admit and live with their own insecurities and learn to live with courage in the face of these anxieties.[54]

Similar to Bugental, Clark Moustakas was influenced throughout his career by the work of Frankl, as well as that of May. Like May, Moustakas received his PhD from Columbia University and began his writing career in the early 1950s. Moustakas was very much interested in existential psychotherapy. While his writing on this subject never reached the popularity of either Frankl or May, Moustakas carved out his own influence in the general field of existential-humanistic psychology by pioneering research methods that can be applied to the noetic dimension of meaning and the unified human experience.

Clark Moustakas developed a formalized phenomenological research method that now allows psychological researchers to examine the human level of experience that Frankl was so concerned about; this approach is known as

"Heuristic research." This form of psychological inquiry provides a guided process of allowing the experience and insights of the researcher to clarify the essence of the phenomenon as they are experienced by people. This requires that the researcher live the question until the question reveals something of its essential nature. This heuristic process goes through six stages: interest, immersion, incubation, illumination, explication, and synthesis. According to Moustakas, "The final step in heuristic presentation and handling of data is the development of a creative synthesis of the experience . . . characterizing the phenomenon."[55] In this way the researcher is able to use an academically accepted method and still communicate the essence of the lived experience.

Another *American friend* of Frankl's approach is Kirk Schneider. Schneider's publishing career began in the early 1990s when he collaborated with Rollo May. Schneider now promotes a method known as the existential-integrative approach to psychotherapy. This reflects Frankl's view of Logotherapy as an adjunct to other therapy; so too existential-integrative denotes that existential insight informs psychotherapy, and the therapist integrates various techniques to fit the needs of the client.

On a theoretical level, Schneider is particularly supportive of Frankl's stance on the importance freedom and responsibility play in helping the individual to make life choices. Schneider is also very keen to acknowledge the importance of the inner subjective life of the client, including issues of embodiment, fantasy, and imagination. Through the exploration of the client's inner life the client is able to take ownership of his own subjective reality. This will undoubtedly bring about some anxiety of authenticity, but the therapist is there to help with the resistance to this anxiety. In this sense then, the therapist helps with *vivification* which involves helping the client recognize that he is resistant to this authenticity because it causes anxiety. Next is *confrontation* which is an amplified version of vivification that calls for the client to respond to this anxiety, by confronting it and courageously overcoming the inner blocks to authenticity.[56]

Ultimately, Schneider views his work of promoting an existential-integrative approach to be one that mirrors Frankl's work with Logotherapy. The goal of humanizing psychotherapy and understanding the whole person is something Schneider notes:

> It is one of the sad ironies of our field that people like Rollo May had to enroll in nonpsychology graduate programs (like those of theology or literature) in order to study the whole person. While some disaffected students eventually come back to psychology's fold, as did Dr. May, how many do not? How much intellectual talent is discouraged by the vested interests of mainstream psychology and the commercialized culture to which it is obliged? But this state of affairs is changing, as this volume attests, and I hope more will welcome it.[57]

What Schneider, May, Bugental, and Moustakas have succeeded in doing is allowing existential thought to inform their practice. The overall goal of these men was to rehumanize psychology and explore how people avoid and deny the existential givens of what it means to be a human being. They responded to Frankl's call to heed the cry for meaning with careers that influenced the theory and practice of psychology.[58]

TORCH BEARERS

While most existential psychotherapists all share some important ideas with Frankl, many others have found his teachings to be truly inspirational. One such individual that has built his career upon, and nurtured the traditions of Frankl, is the Canadian Psychologist Dr. Paul T. P. Wong and his wife Dr. Lillian Wong. As founder and president of the *International Network for Personal Meaning*, and its academic arm, the *International Society for Existential Psychotherapy and Positive Psychology*, Wong has remained true to Frankl's ideals.

The key points from Frankl that Wong stresses are the importance of meaning, the reality of ultimate meaning, and the inherent spirituality of the person. Like Frankl, he has lived a life melding together issues of spirituality (serving as the pastor of an ethnic Chinese congregation) and academic psychotherapeutic training (including founding a graduate program in counseling psychology at a Canadian university). Although retired, he continues to offer training institutes and organizes conferences, as well as publishes books and journals focused on existential psychotherapy. He also provides training institutes on his version of Frankl's Logotherapy, calling it *meaning centered therapy*.[59]

Within Wong's meaning centered therapy training sessions, he begins by looking at the big questions of life, examining the narrative of what makes life meaningful. Through this introduction, he teaches about the possible trajectories that life may take, and how one can choose to deal with the struggles of life. Part of this is examining false beliefs that we may buy into and that steal our power of choice. He then highlights how to live properly, through Frankl's understanding of self-transcendence, service, and commitment. Wong then adds to Frankl's ideas of responsibility and purpose, by including themes of understanding and enjoyment: his P.U.R.E. principle of living: **P**urpose, **U**nderstanding, **R**esponsibility, and **E**njoyment.[60]

This principle is then made personal, as each individual is asked to explore his life in a way that helps to clarify individual passion and purpose. It is an exploration and choosing of those things that we can do in our limited lifespan to make a difference. The course then deepens this by moving from the, *what* of passions and purpose, to the *how*, exploring ideas of courage, self-knowledge, human understanding, and approaches to problem-solving. Of course, Wong keeps true to Frankl's tenets, so that like Frankl, Wong returns to examining the essential experience of responsibility, and doing the right thing to support life. Following Frankl, Wong sees this as being a pathway of spirituality and responsibility.

While Viktor Frankl is no longer with us, his legacy of meaning remains, so long as we still have leaders within our midst that carry on the tradition of his life and work. Research continues to deepen our understanding. Under the direction of competent leaders like Paul T. P. Wong the call to maintain the humanness of the client is heard far and wide. It appears that Frankl's light of meaning still burns bright, casting out the darkness of mere being.

Another important torch bearer of Frankl is Elizabeth Lukas; someone who not only continues to follow the principles of Frankl, she even identifies herself as a logotherapist. Her ardent efforts to continue to promote and develop Frankl's Logotherapy makes her the most important modern figure in perpetuating Frankl's ideals and practices as he conceived of them. A student of Frankl himself, Elizabeth Lukas received her PhD from the University of Vienna and has spent her career (mostly in Germany) since the early 1970s in the training, promotion, and practice of Logotherapy.

Within Lukas' vision of Logotherapy, the same essential principles set out by Frankl remain true today. The most basic of these principles is that meaning can be found in all circumstances. However, the therapist must remember that it is useful to lead clients toward areas where they may experience meaning. For example, this experience of meaning may be found in one's own uniqueness, where one has unique traits, talents, a special situation, or network of relationships that makes the individual irreplaceable. Another frame for experiencing meaning is in choice, the freedom to choose not only actions but also attitudes within situations. There is also the area of responsibility, where one chooses to act in line with responsibility. Finally, there is the principle of self-transcendence, where one is called to include others in their own interests and to expend effort in the care of the interests of others.[61]

According to Lukas, people with emotional wellness are able to assimilate their previous experience with their present and future prospects. Emotionally disturbed individuals, by contrast, have a propensity to focus either on a fragment of their past experience, or, on their future expectations, to the extent of ignoring the continuity of their experience. An over emphasis upon negative past experiences, or future concerns or expectations, can then result in a person ignoring their present being. In response to this tendency, modern Logotherapy offers some practical guidelines to recapture the meaning of the present moment.

The first step is to help the client examine his life in terms of *gifts received*, taking an inventory of blessings within life. In so doing one explores the possibilities of life and can view the present as an opportunity to choose how to react to present possibilities. The second phase is to identify a task to do in the present that is in line with *a call* the client has in his life. The third step is to be aware of *abilities and resources* for completing this task in the present, making a strategic plan. The fourth stride is then *committing* to the action plan and carrying it out. It is here that the client graduates to work outside of the therapy office, for this is something that the client must do alone.[62]

Within the counseling relationship proper, including when Logotherapy is used, there are three phases: assessment, treatment, and follow-up. During the assessment phase, the therapist establishes therapeutic rapport and the problem is explored and defined. For the logotherapist, this includes gathering information within the context of the client's life and experience with meaning. At this stage the standard information gathering procedures of interviews, questionnaires, and mental status examination, all apply. However, the logotherapist may wish to also gather information regarding the client's current life satisfaction, existential frustrations, sense of freedom, ability to make and commit to choices, as well as an overall sense of calling and responsibility.

Once the issues have been clarified within the counseling relationship, a therapeutic treatment plan can be developed. This may take the form of focusing on the one presenting problem, or dealing with both a focused and wider life-plan treatment. When Logotherapy is appropriate there are some typical strategies that may be used within treatment. The first step in this logotherapeutic process then is normally to help the client recognize that he is more than a collection of symptoms and problems; he is a human being capable of a meaningful existence.

In a case such as anxiety or depression this helps the client to create a sense of distance from the symptoms. In essence this first step is Frankl's de-reflection. This first movement helps the client to recognize that the self is more than a collection of fears, failures, or insecurities that he or she is able to make choices, to choose directions, and to discover meaning. In learning to define the self as more than the problem, the client is then in a place of empowerment. The client can draw upon personal spiritual resources to begin to change subjective experiences.[63]

This distancing then allows the client to begin working on changing personal attitudes. Since the emotion of the problem is no longer overwhelming the client, the client can reconsider attitudes toward the problem in the wider context of life. Here the therapist facilitates the client by asking open and reflexive questions to discover new attitudes and meanings. Oftentimes these meanings are not new to the client, but the client simply failed to consider them when formulating their initial reaction to the problem. When there is successful de-reflection and modification of attitudes, there is typically also symptom reduction.

Then comes the latter part of the logotherapeutic portion of treatment, where the client develops an orientation toward a chosen meaning. This is not a purely intellectual exercise. This involves the client formulating concrete strategies to serve this new meaningful direction and making concrete choices. These choices then allow the client to practice his new meaningful living strategies outside of the therapy office. In so doing the logotherapeutic relationship makes the transition to a more supportive and follow-up role, finally closing out the therapeutic relationship.[64]

Though modern Logotherapy remains more of a humanizing approach than a set of protocols and procedures; it does retain a few specific therapeutic techniques. The two primary techniques were first practiced by Frankl and are most often described in the context of anxiety-related disorders. The first of these is *de-reflection*, which has already been discussed. It is based upon the principle of self-transcendence, drawing on the innate human capacity to distance the self from external and internal conditions and to reach beyond the self. The second technique is *paradoxical intention*, based on Frankl's discovery that phobias are best dealt with by intending to the fear. The principle is that an intended action can displace a fear, for one cannot fear what one direct intends to happen. This intending behavior then breaks the vicious cycle of anticipatory anxiety.[65]

Within modern Logotherapy however, Lukas does provide a caution about using these techniques. The caution is that due diligence must first be done in the assessment phase to ensure and establish that the disturbance being treated does not have a physiological cause.[66] Once it is established, through appropriate assessment and referrals that the roots lie in the client's exaggerated hyper-intention, then the logotherapeutic techniques may be applied. It should also be noted that in modern Logotherapy, the therapist does not choose the specific content of the particular technique. Rather, the therapist explains to the client the connection between the symptoms and the role of de-reflection or paradoxical intention as one possible way to break this pattern. Once the client chooses the content of the particular technique and symptom reduction is experienced, the therapist can then facilitate movement to the next step in therapy. This would be the movement of the client toward a choosing and enacting of meaningful tasks.[67]

While these techniques were formulated originally by Frankl, he himself was impressed by the way that Lukas used them within her modern practice. He even makes mention of them in his writings, quoting from specific case files of Lukas.[68] Frankl also notes how Lukas has created innovations within the field of assessment in service of Logotherapy. What is particularly important to modern Logotherapy is Lukas' primary contribution in terms of techniques, namely *The Appealing Technique*. In so doing Lukas adds a more client-centered approach to Logotherapy while acknowledging that conditions sometimes block the ability of the person to grasp meaning. This may be the case for someone with an endogenous depression or severe addiction requiring detoxification. In such cases, the client simply expresses dignity for the client's meaning-orientation while acknowledging that the client's subjective sense of meaning and freedom is currently blocked. Nevertheless there is an appeal to accomplish self-chosen tasks.

In terms of communications with the client, there is a counter to the client's tendency to blame their condition on a particular context or event. When the client has self-talk that is "I am like this BECAUSE OF that . . ." the appealing technique calls the therapist to invite the client to reframe that self-talk narrative to an "although" statement. Along the lines of, "Although my life was difficult growing up, I have the capacity to live a decent life." In so doing, Lukas' technique helps the client to retain authorship of their personal story and provides a way to help the client re-author their story in a different direction.

Today, Logotherapy continues to have a place within the world of counseling and psychotherapy.[69] Thanks to the work of such torch bearers as Elizabeth Lukas and Paul T. P. Wong, the ideals of Frankl continue to be researched, discussed, developed, and practiced. The goal of Logotherapy, to rehumanize psychotherapy, has been joined by other existentially oriented therapists, and a trend moves toward integration of various schools to better meet the needs of the client as a whole person. This trend is truly in line with Frankl's overall hope for psychotherapy, to honor the innate dignity of clients.

CONCLUDING REFLECTIONS

Viktor Frankl and his concept of Logotherapy have brought much to the field of psychotherapy. Most notable is his melding of a philosophical, phenomenological, and hermeneutical anthropology that recognizes the existential being of humanity. Frankl's logotherapeutic techniques of paradoxical intention, de-reflection, and the use of humor also endure within mainstream psychotherapy. Finally, Logotherapy's call for self-transcendence, as the crux of human existence, opens the door to help people understand happiness. Yet, for all of his professional impact on the field of psychiatry, his influence goes much deeper.

Frankl calls us to recognize man for what he can be, not simply what man is. He reminds us that all people have a "will to meaning," and a desire for significance. Everyone longs to find a personal identity, to experience a meaning within and for existence. To find direction in life, a worthwhile cause to serve, something or someone to love. It is a reminder that we must never forget our own humanness, nor be lost in our own fragile successes; either individually or as a society.

On the noetic level then, the affluence of Western society may fulfill physical needs, but Frankl reminds us that it does not necessarily fulfill our need for meaning. The pressures of life have increased in proportion to abundance, so the man in the street gets caught in a dysfunctional cycle in order to keep going. Through a combination of self-indulgence, substance abuse, and escapist entertainment – we are escapees from ourselves. In living the good life we miss what is more valuable, the meaningful life.

Frankl also reminds us of an essential grounding of existence, namely God. That we are beings that are dependent upon God and aware of our role set out by God through our conscience. That ultimately we are not the measure of all things, and are responsible to God. This essential spirituality frames the grounding of existence, of meaning, and ultimately of what it means to be a human being. It means that while we are physical, that is not all that we are. It reminds us that we are dimensionally complex; we are interdependent, caring, loving, creatures of God. We have a freedom to make choices and a responsibility to engage life. Through this commitment, we can experience a temporal reward in the experience of meaning, and this infuses life with a joy that transcends external circumstances.

Frankl reminds us that part of living is to take, what Kierkegaard called, "the leap of faith." This is not to say that we must blindly believe, but simply that there are some things in life that are unknowable intellectually, but require a response from life existentially. As Frankl says,

> True, it is not possible to find out intellectually whether everything is ultimately meaningless or whether there is ultimate meaning behind everything. But if we cannot answer the question intellectually we may do so existentially. Where an intellectual cognition fails an existential decision is due . . . believing is not at all some sort of thinking *minus* the reality of that which is thought, believing is rather some sort of thinking *plus* something, namely, the existentiality of him or her who does the thinking.[70]

This call to an existential spirituality is what I believe, sets Frankl apart from his peers. Whatever makes Frankl's contributions distinct, his legacy continues to improve the lives of people, even in the unfixable moments of existence. For there will always be situations of suffering, but where there is meaning, despair is banished.

NOTES

1. Melvin Kimble, ed., *Viktor Frankl's Contribution to Spirituality and Aging* (Binghampton, N.Y.: Hawthorn Pastoral Press, 2000), 1–4.

2. By applying Csikszentmihalyi's systems model we can better understand how the total dedication of Frankl to Logotherapy helped propel him to greatness.

M. Csikszentmihalyi, "Creativity across the life-span: A systems view." In. *Talent Development* (New York: Gifted Psychology Press, 1995), 9–18.

3. M. Csikszentmihalyi, *Flow: The Psychology of Optimal Experience* (New York: Harper & Row, 1990).

4. M. Csikszentmihalyi, "Creativity across the life-span: A systems view." In. *Talent Development* (New York: Gifted Psychology Press, 1995), 9–18.

5. These creative individuals anticipate what others will say when they see or hear their own new ideas. In all of the fields we studied, individuals are very aware of what colleagues and other people in their field are doing, thinking, and what their concerns are. It is very rare to find the isolated creator that a romantic version of history has told us exists – the kind of persons who never talk to anyone and work all by themselves. That is not really typical at all. Most creative people, even if they don't interact with others, have internalized the criteria of the other people in the field, their opinions, and values. Of course, the creative person may then decide to reject everything that the field believes in, but the rejection will have no effect unless it is done in a way that is acceptable to others.

M. Csikszentmihalyi, "Creativity across the life-span: A systems view." In. *Talent Development* (New York: Gifted Psychology Press, 1995), 9–18.

6. As Csikszentmihalyi attests, "These simple truths about the flexibility of the person are important components within an individual who changes their field: What kind of person is the one who does all this? One way to talk about the individuals we studied, is that they demonstrate something which I call a complex personality. Ordinarily, psychologists talk about people being either extroverted or introverted, masculine or feminine, being cooperative or cooperating. What we found in our study is the amazing ability on the part of creative people to move across the whole spectrum so that they don't generally end up at one of the extremes in the distribution of traits. That is why I call it complexity: an integration of different abilities." M. Csikszentmihalyi, "Creativity across the life-span: A systems view," 9–18.

7. G. Colvin, ed. *Talent is Over-Rated* (New York: Penguin, 2008), 5–50.

8. Ibid.

9. Ibid.

10. Klingberg, *When Life Calls Out to Us*, 285.

11. Frankl, *Man's Search for Ultimate Meaning,* 3–45.

12. Ibid.

13. Ibid., 18.

14. Frankl, *Man's Search for Ultimate Meaning*, 29.

15. Ibid.

16. As Redsand notes:

When he was thirteen, Viktor Frankl was declared a man at his bar mitzvah ceremony in a Vienna synagogue. At eighty-three, he chose to celebrate a second bar mitzvah at the Western Well in Jerusalem. It is a joyful time in Jewish tradition when someone has lived seventy years beyond his first bar mitzvah at thirteen and chooses to celebrate his commitment to Jewish law and life once again. Wearing his prayer shawl and his father's phylacteries, Viktor listened and repeated the sacred texts with the rabbi. As the rabbi went on, Viktor kept saying to himself, "How beautiful, how beautiful."

Viktor Frankl's second bar mitzvah was only one indication of the depth of his commitment to his faith. He didn't often talk about it because he felt that faith is something private. But from the time of his release from Turkheim, he prayed the Shema Yisrael every day. He also prayed his own prayers. After the Holocaust, if something bad happened to him, he imagined himself on his knees and gave thanks "to heaven that this is the worst thing that happened to me today."

After his losses and the horrors he suffered in the Holocaust, Viktor Frankl allowed himself to get irritated about life's small annoyances, but he refused to complain about the big problems that came his way. For example, once while he was staying at an Alpine lodge, planning an early morning climb, people in the bar below were having a loud party. Viktor finally went downstairs and yelled at them to be quiet so he could get some sleep. However, even when he became blind at the age of eighty-five, as Elly said, "Viktor lived what he talked – absolutely. . . . Never did he complain about his blindness. Not even once."

Anna Redsand, *Viktor Frankl: A Life Worth Living* (New York: Clarion, 2006), 128.

17. Klingberg, *When Life Calls Out To Us,* 200–268.

18. Frankl, *Man's Search for Meaning,* 135.

19. Ibid.

20. Frankl, *The Doctor and the Soul*, 3.

21. It should be noted that some will argue that Frankl does not go into adequate depth in fleshing out the relationship between freedom and responsibility. It must be recognized that Frankl does not go to the lengths of Sartre in recognizing the value of freedom as possibility for example. As Sartre argues, one is free to choose to kill another in infinite transcendence; or free to love another in finite transcendence. As such, responsibility comes on the scene insofar as one limits his abstract freedom its concrete ethical or "existential" place in responsibility as facticity. By giving one's situation a positive meaning (such as ethical actions are limited to love or to the good), rather than a negative meaning (or evil) one limits freedom.

22. Frankl, *Man's Search for Ultimate Meaning*, 118–155.

23. Frankl, *The Doctor and the Soul*, xxiv.

24. Alexander Vesely, *Viktor and I.* Noetic Films: Laguna Niguel, California.

25. Frankl, *The Will to Meaning*, 18.

26. Frankl, *Man's Search for Ultimate Meaning,* 37.

27. Ibid., 60.

28. Ibid., 36–45.

29. Ibid.

30. Klingberg, *When Life Calls Out to Us,* 338–334.

31. Redsand, *Viktor Frankl*, 132 shares the vividness of this difficult experience for Frankl:

In October 1996, Viktor answered the phone in his study, and after he hung up, Elly heard an outcry from his room. His niece had just told him that his sister, Stella, had died in Australia. That evening, Viktor was admitted to the hospital. He had already been in the hospital several times for heart problems. But after Stella's death, his health seemed to get much worse.

32. Redsand, *Viktor Frankl*, 133.

33. Ibid., 134.

34. Irvin Yalom, *Existential Psychotherapy* (New York: Basic Books, 1980), 10–320.

35. Ibid., 442.

36. Ibid.

37. Ibid., 463.

38. Ibid., 423.

39. Ibid., 463.

40. Ibid., 423.

41. Ibid., 470.

42. Ibid., 468.

43. Klingberg, *When Life Calls Out to Us*, 242.

44. Yalom, *Existential Psychotherapy*, 442.

45. Frankl, *The Will to Meaning*, 10.

46. Mick Cooper, *Existential Therapies* (London: Sage, 2003), 35–50.

47. Ibid.

48. E. Straus *Phenomenological Psychology* (New York, Basic Books, 1966), 1–22.

49. Eugen Minkowski. *Lived Time: Phenomenological and Psychopathological Studies* (Evanston, IL: Northwestern University Press, 1970), 11–29.

50. Eugen Minkowski, *Findings in a case of schizophrenic depression.* IN: May, R., Angel, E., and Ellenberger, H (eds). *Existence* (New York: Basic Books), 132.

51. Ibid., 134.

52. Rollo May became known as the "Father of Existential Psychology in America" according to Hoeller, K. "Introduction" Review of Existential Psychology and Psychiatry, 24 (1999): v–vii.

53. Rollo May, *Love and Will* (New York: Norton, 1969), 228.

54. James Bugental, *Psychotherapy and Process: The Fundamentals of an Existential-Humanistic Psychotherapy* (San Francisco: Jossey-Bass), 120–130.

55. Clark Moustakas, *Heuristic Research: Design, Methodology, and Applications* (London: Sage, 1990), 52.

56. Mick Cooper, Existential Therapies (London: Sage, 2003), 70.

57. A footnote comment in: Kirk Schneider, Existential – Integrative Psychotherapy (New York: Routledge, 2008), 9.

58. In the final lines of Frankl's first book *The Doctor and the Soul*, 301, he issued a challenge to change psychotherapy, "For too long the cry has remained unheard. But a psychotherapy that sets out "on its way to rehumanization" should listen to the unheard cry for meaning." In this light, Rollo May, James Bugental, Clark Moustakas, and Kirk Schneider can all be considered "friends" of Frankl's approach to psychotherapy.

59. In April, 2014 Wong announced that his organization was approved by the Frankl Institute of Vienna to offer training in Logotherapy.

60. Wong, Paul, Meaning Centred Therapy (Toronto: International Society for Existential Psychotherapy, 2007). http://www.meaning.ca/therapy/MCT_articles.htm.

61. These principles are put into a fuller context within, Elizabeth Lukas *Meaningful Living* (New York: Grove, 1984).

62. The principles set forth here are based upon Elizabeth Lukas 1994 book *Psychotherapie im Wurde* (*Psychotherapy with Dignity*) as summarized by Maria Unger's dissertation *Viktor E. Frankl's Meaning-oriented Approach to Counselling Psychology* (Edmonton, Alberta: University of Alberta, 1999), 118–119.

63. More information is available in Elizabeth Lukas *Meaning in Suffering: Comfort in crisis in Logotherapy* (Berkeley, CA: Institute of Logotherapy Press, 1986).

64. This process was summarized by Maria Unger, based upon Lukas *Psychotherapie in Wurde: Sinnorientierte Lebenshilfe nach Viktor E. Frankl* (1994), 180–190.

65. Viktor Frankl, *The Unheard Cry for Meaning*, 150–157.

66. Further discussion on this may be found in Elizabeth Lukas' book, *Meaning in suffering: Comfort in crisis through Logotherapy.*

67. Elizabeth Lukas, "Modification of attitudes," *The International Forum for Logotherapy,* 3, 25–34.

68. In Frankl's book, *The Unheard Cry for Meaning*, he makes note of Lukas' work on pages 25, 31, 34, 41 & 148, highlighting her innovations in assessment and clinical use of classical logotherapeutic techniques in treatment.

69. Much research on happiness, meaning, and psychometric measures of meaning in life continue to be studied, in the tradition pioneered by Frankl. Discussions of some of these are included in the appendix.

70. Frankl, *Man's Search for Ultimate Meaning*, 146.

Glossary

Alienation According to Frankl, alienation concerns the break in; this may be with others, with our social group, or our emotions.

Anthropology The anthropology of Frankl's Logotherapy was one that included the wholeness of the person as a physical, psychical, and spiritual being.

Appealing technique Appealing technique within modern Logotherapy consists of suggestions to direct the client toward new and positive thinking.

Attitudinal values Attitudinal paradigm within modern Logotherapy refers to a person's capacity to transcend unavoidable suffering brought about by an unchangeable fate. That through a chosen attitude of courage, unavoidable suffering is transformed into a heroic and victorious achievement where despair is banished.

Boredom According to Logotherapy, the experience of boredom is a lack of interest in engaging the world. This comes about through a lack of meaning to incite engagement.

Conscience According to Logotherapy, the conscience is not simply an internal voice but is a transcendent quality of the psyche that connects man to God and may not be reduced to mere socialization.

Creative value Creative value within modern Logotherapy refers to the realm where a person creates a work or performs a deed.

Death According to Logotherapy, death is a theme that frames a person's existence. It is part of life, and any life that is lived must also include death. To live an authentic existence then one must take death into account.

De-reflection De-reflection in modern Logotherapy is a technique that turns attention away from a negative situation to focus on something positive.

Despair According to Logotherapy, despair is the most unpleasant of experiences. It is suffering without meaning.

Existential Existential refers to human existence itself, or to the meaning of existence, or to the striving to find concrete meaning in personal existence.

Experiential value The experiential value within modern Logotherapy refers to the realm where one experiences a value or encounters someone.

Finitude Finitude within the logotherapeutic framework of Viktor Frankl means that man is amazing, but also limited in his ability to understand and grasp certain concepts or achieve certain goals. There is an aspect of human existence where man must accept his existential finiteness that he will fail, he will suffer, and he will die.

Happiness Happiness is an interesting concept within Logotherapy that is experienced when a person engages in living a responsible life. The pursuit of happiness then amounts to a self-contradiction. For the more we strive for happiness, the less we attain it. Happiness rather is an experience that ensues from engaging the world. It cannot be pursued successfully. The very pursuit of happiness thwarts its aim.

Happiness in Logotherapy is viewed as a side effect of living out the self-transcendent qualities of existence. Once one has served a cause or is involved in loving another human being, happiness occurs by itself.

Hyper-reflection Hyper-reflection within Logotherapy is essentially when the client pays an inordinate amount of attention to something. Typically this abundance of attention results in some dysfunction.

Logotherapy Logotherapy is a branch of existential psychology that offers therapy through meaning. It typically refers to the therapeutic works of Viktor E. Frankl.

Meaning Within Logotherapy meaning typically refers to the subjective experience of understanding and action converging within human experience. That is, according to Frankl meaning is best experienced through doing, rather than merely philosophizing. Objective meanings may not always be grasped, though they undoubtedly exist. Meanings are not so much constructed by the individual as discovered by the individual. This makes Logotherapy different from many purely constructivist paradigms.

Meaning is objective. It is real, that is, outside or independent of the person, whether or not he perceives life to be meaningful. Meaning is "out there" in the world to be found by each individual. Meaning is discovered, because it is real. It is not invented by each person. The outside dimension of reality fulfills something inside the human person. There is a direct or one-to-one correspondence between the subject, that is, each human person, and the objective, that is, the person or thing out in the world, which fulfills him.

Noetic The psychical and spiritual components of man.

Noological dimension According to logotherapeutic theory, the noological dimension is those dimensional layers of man that are uniquely human and provide a unity of person.

Noodynamics Noodynamics refers to the tension between what people have already achieved and what they still ought to accomplish.

Noogenic Noogenic has to do with the spiritual dimension of human personality.

Paradoxical intention Paradoxical intention is a logotherapeutic technique by which clients are encouraged to do or wish the very thing they fear.

Phenomenology In Viktor E. Frankl's view phenomenology is the study of human experience. According to his view the phenomenology of the man in the street reveals three key values that must be engaged within life: creative, experiential, and attitudinal.

Problems in perceiving life's meaning Problems in perceiving life's meaning do not mean life is meaningless according to Logotherapy. Meaning is a given, a first principle. Meaning is a fundamental premise to something basic to life itself. One may question the meaning of life. One may even despair over the meaning of life. But it does not mean that meaning is not really there. Rather, it only means that the person fails to perceive it or is blind to it, because of existential problems.

Psychogenic neuroses Psychogenic neuroses refer to the conflicts between drives and instincts within the human psyche.

Self-detachment In Logotherapy it is the ability of man to reflect back and interact with the self. By virtue of self-detachment, man is capable of joking about himself, laughing at himself, and ridiculing his own fears.

Self-transcendence One must discover and encounter meaning by engaging the world through loving and experiencing in acts of responsibility. The fulfillment of man only comes not in self-actualization, but in forgetting the self and immersing the self in service. In transcending the self, man fulfills his essence of existence and experiences happiness.

Within logotherapeutic theory, being human is being always directed, and pointing, to something or someone other than oneself: to a meaning to fulfill or another human being to encounter, a cause to serve or a person to love. Only to the extent that someone is living out this self-transcendence of human existence is he truly human or does become his true self. He becomes so not by concerning himself with his self-actualization, but by forgetting himself and giving himself, overlooking himself and focusing outward.

A human being finds himself only to the extent to which he loses himself in the first place, be it for the sake of something or somebody, for the sake of a cause or a fellowman, or for God's sake.

Socratic dialogue The Socratic dialogue elicits solutions clients intuitively have by clarifying their feelings, goals, and commitments.

Spirituality Frankl uses a German word to describe the spiritual aspects or spiritual realms of man: "By . . . Geist . . . we mean the core or nucleus of the personality." It encompasses the very act of man's own self-transcendence in living out and discovers meaning.

Suffering Within Logotherapy suffering is an unavoidable aspect of life. Suffering without meaning brings despair, but within suffering there is an opportunity to encounter meaning. Life can be meaningful through the stand we take toward suffering.

Suicide Logotherapy teaches that suicide may be caused by a feeling of meaninglessness and that its prevention accordingly presupposes that the patient discover a meaning to life.

Survival Logotherapy teaches that meaning has real survival value. Survival is dependent upon direction. However, survival cannot be the supreme value. Unless life points to something beyond itself, survival is pointless and meaningless. It is not even possible. This is the lesson that Frankl learned in the Nazi concentration camps. Only those who were oriented toward the future, toward a goal in the future, and toward a meaning to fulfill in the future were likely to survive.

Tension Logotherapy teaches that an amount of emotional tension is helpful for life. The tension aroused by a meaning to fulfill is inherent in being human and is indispensable for mental well-being. When man needs first of all is that tension which is created by direction.

Transitoriness In Logotherapy transitoriness refers to the every changing nature of life, where the future does not yet exist and the past is left behind. The only thing that really exists is the present. The challenge is to find meaning in the ever changing process of coming into being. The way this is done is through seeing life as changing possibilities into realities. The future is full of possibilities and as a person lives life he transforms these possibilities into realities locked in the past.

Ultimate meaning In Logotherapy ultimate meaning refers to the ungraspable meaning that provides a context for life but is known only to God. It was Frankl's contention that faith in the ultimate meaning is preceded by trust in an ultimate being, by trust in God. There is an existential or day-to-day meaning in one's life to sustain a person in the here and now, in this life. But there is also an ultimate meaning, which gives meaning not only to a person's overall life but also his moment-by-moment life. This ultimate meaning infuses the day-to-day meaning of a person's life.

Within Logotherapy, the ultimate meaning of life is grounded in the Eternal, the ground of being. Such meaning is glimpsed dimly through knowing, loving, and serving God. In shore, ultimate meaning comes from believing in God and trusting in his ultimate goodness. Only an ultimate being is worthy of a person's ultimate commitment in life.

Unconscious The unconscious in logotherapeutic theory is the experience of existence because the foundation of existence cannot be fully reflected upon and thus cannot be fully aware of itself. The unconscious is the center of the human person in his very depth and is unreflective.

Values Values are central to logotherapeutic theory as they are conceptual frameworks that hold meaning that is released when man engages life. There are three groups of values that reveal meaning that a person can encounter. The key values are a deed we do, an experience, encounter, or a love expressed, and a stance toward an unchangeable fate.

Viennese schools of psychotherapy The first Viennese school of psychotherapy is Freudian Psychoanalytic Psychology, the second is Adlerian Individual Psychology, and the third is Frankl's Logotherapy.

World view (Weltanschauung) According to Logotherapy there is a constructed nature to the subjective world we live within. So too, there is no psychotherapy without a theory of man and a philosophy of life underlying it. Logotherapy is based upon an explicit philosophy of life that is connected by three main principles: (1) freedom of will, (2) will to meaning, and (3) meaning of life.

Bibliography

Asher, L. "Paradoxical Intention: A review of preliminary research," *The International Forum for Logotherapy*, 1 (1979): 18–21.

Bazzi, T. "Paradoxical Intention and Autogenic Training," *The International Forum for Logotherapy,* 2 no. 2, (1979): 35–37.

Berry, R. *Freud: A Beginner's Guide*. London: Hodder and Stoughton.

Cannon, B. *Sartre and Psychoanalysis: An Existentialist Challenge*. Kansas City, KS: University Press of Kansas, 1991.

Collins, G. *The Rebuilding of Psychology: An Integration of Psychology and Christianity*. Wheaton, Ill.: Tyndale House, 1989.

Colvin, G. ed. *Talent is Over-Rated*. New York: Penguin, 2008.

Corey, G. *Theory and Practice of Counseling and Psychotherapy*. Belmont, CA: Brooks/Cole, 2013.

Crumbaugh, J. *Seeking of Noetic Goals Test Manual*. Munster, Indiana: Psychometric Affiliates, 1977.

Crumbaugh, J. and Henrion, R. "PIL Test: Administration, Interpretation, Uses Theory and Critique." *The International Forum for Logotherapy*, 11, no. 2 (1988): 847–853.

Crumbaugh, J "The Seeking of Noetic Goals Test (SONG): A Complementary Scale to the Purpose in Life Test (PIL)." *Journal of Clinical Psychology* 33 (1977): 900–907.

Csikszentmihalyi, M. "Creativity across the life-span: A systems view." In *Talent Development.* New York: Gifted Psychology Press, 1995.

Csikszentmihalyi, M. *Flow: The Psychology of Optimal Experience*. New York: Harper & Row, 1990.

Fabry, J. B. *The Pursuit of Meaning*. Berkeley, CA: Institute of Logotherapy Press, 1987.

Frankl, Viktor. *Psychotherapy and Existentialism: Selected Papers on Logotherapy*. New York: Simon & Schuster, 1967.

Frankl, Viktor. *The Unheard Cry for Meaning*. New York: Simon & Schuster, 1978.

Frankl, Viktor. *Man's Search for Meaning*. New York: Pocket Books, 1984.
Frankl, Viktor. *The Doctor and the Soul*. New York: Vintage Books, 1986.
Frankl, Viktor. *The Will to Meaning*. New York: Penguin, 1988.
Frankl, Viktor. *Recollections: An Autobiography*. Cambridge, MA: Basic, 2000.
Frankl, Viktor. *Man's Search for Ultimate Meaning*. New York: Basic, 2000.
Fowler, James. *The Stages of Faith: The Psychology of Human Development and the Quest for Meaning*. San Francisco: Harper Collins, 1981.
Freud, Sigmund. "Three Essays on the Theory of Sexuality," in *The Freud Reader*, ed. Peter Gay. London: Norton, 1989.
Freud, Sigmund. "The Future of an Illusion," in *The Freud Reader*, ed. Peter Gay. London: Norton, 1989.
Freud, Sigmund. "The Ego and the Id." In Peter Gay. *The Freud Reader*. London: Norton, 1989.
Gould, William. *Frankl: Life with Meaning*. Belmont: Brooks/Cole, 1993.
Gressel, J. *Development of the Jewish Faith*. Berkeley: Unpublished Manuscript, 2010.
Guttmann, D. *Finding Meaning in Life, at Mid-Life and Beyond: Wisdom and Spirit from Logotherapy*. Westport, CT: Praeger, 2008
Heidegger, Martin. *Being and Time*. New York, NY: Harper, 1962.
Heller, S. *Freud: A to Z*. New York: John Wiley and Sons, 2005.
Hutzell, R. R. "A Review of the Purpose in Life Test." *The International Forum for Logotherapy* 11 (1988): 89–101.
Hutzell, R. R. "Overview of Research Published in The International Forum for Logotherapy." *The International Forum for Logotherapy* 23 (2000): 111–115.
Hutzell, R. R. & Peterson, T. J. "An MMPI Existential Vacuum Scale for Logotherapy Research." *The International Forum for Logotherapy* 8, no. 2 (1985): 97–100.
Jastrzebski, A. "Toward a Better Understanding of the Philosophy of Psychology." *History and Philosophy of Psychology* 14 no.1 (2012), 13–33.
Jones, Ernest. *The life and work of Sigmund Freud*. New York: Basic Books, 1957.
Kashdan, T, Gallager, M., Silvia, P., Winterstein, B., Breen, W. E., Terhar, D., & Steger, M. F "The Curiosity and Exploration Inventory – II: Development, factor structure, and initial psychometrics," *Journal of Research in Personality*, 43 (2009): 987–998.
Kimble, Melvin ed., *Viktor Frankl's Contribution to Spirituality and Aging*. Binghampton, N.Y.: Hawthorn Pastoral Press, 2000.
Klingberg, H. *When Life Calls Out to Us*. New York: Doubleday, 2001.
Krell, D. F. ed. *Basic Writings: Martin Heidegger*. London: Routledge, 2009.
Lavine, T. Z. *From Socrates to Sartre*. New York, NY: Bantam Books, 1984.
Lent, T. *Viktor E. Frankl Anthology*. Bloomington, IN: Xlibris Publishing, 2004.
Lester, A. *Hope in Pastoral Care and Counseling*. Louisville, KY: Westminster John Knox Press, 1995.
Lukas, E. "A Validation of Logotherapy." *The International Forum for Logotherapy* 4, no. 2 (1981): 116–125.
Lukas, E. & Peeble, J. *Logotest Manual*. Saratoga, CA: Institute of Logotherapy, 1989.

Lyubomirsky, S. & Lepper, H. S. "A Measure of Subjective Happiness: Preliminary Reliability and Construct Validation," *Social Indicators Research* 46 (1999): 137–155.

McCullogh, M. E., Emmons, R. A., & Tsang, J. "The Grateful Disposition: A Conceptual and Empirical Topography," *Journal of Personality and Social Psychology*, 82 (2002): 112–127.

McLaren, N. "Kandel's New Science of Mind for Psychiatry and the Limits of Reductionism: A critical review," *Ethical Human Psychology and Psychiatry,* 10, 2, (2008): 109–121.

Naylor, T., Willimon, W., & Osterberg, R. *The Search for Meaning in the Workplace.* Nashville: Abingdon, 1996.

Ponsaran, A. "The Philosophical Foundations of Viktor Frankl's Logotherapy." *Philippiniana Sacra* 42, no. 125 (2007): 339–354.

Paolucci, H. *Hegel: On the Arts.* New York, NY: Frederick Ungar Publishing, 1979.

Pattakos, A. *A Prisoner of Our Thoughts: Viktor Frankl's Principles at Work.* San Francisco, CA: Berrett-Koehler, 2004.

Redsand, A. *Viktor Frankl: A Life Worth Living.* New York, NY: Clarion Books, 2006.

Sartre, Jean Paul. *Being and Nothingness.* New York, NY: Washington Square Press, 1992.

Sartre, Jean Paul. *Existentialism is a Humanism.* New Haven, CT: Yale University Press, 2007.

Snyder, C., Harris, C., Anderson, J., Holleran, S., Irving, L., Sigmon, S. "The Will and the Ways: Development and Validation of an Individual-Differences Measure of Hope," *Journal of Personality and Social Psychology* 60 (1991): 570–585.

Spiegelberg, H. *Phenomenology in Psychology and Psychiatry: A Historical Introduction.* Evanston, Ill.: Northwestern University Press, 1972.

Stefanics, C. "Experiences with Logotherapy: Nursing the Elderly." *The International Forum for Logotherapy* 19, no. 1 (1996): 34–38.

Steger, M., Frasier, P., Oishi, S., Kahler, M. "The Meaning in Life Questionnaire: Assessing the Presence and Search for Meaning in Life," *Journal of Counseling Psychology*, 53, no. 1 (2006): 80–93.

Stewart and Mickunas. *Exploring Phenomenology: A Guide to the Field and its Literature.* Athens, OH: Ohio University Press, 1990.

Storr, Anthony. *Freud: A Very Short Introduction.* New York, NY: Oxford, 1989.

Ungar, M. "A Four-Step Model of Logotherapy." *The International Forum for Logotherapy* 20, no. 2 (1997): 113–119.

Wadsworth, T. M. "Logotherapy and 12-Step Programs in Substance Abuse." *The International Forum for Logotherapy* 15 (1992): 13–21.

Wollman, N. "Jung and Freud compared on two types of reductionism." *Journal of Analytical Psychology,* 27 (1982): 149–161.

Wong, P. T. "Meaning-Centered Counseling: A Cognitive – Behavioral Approach to Logotherapy." *The International Forum for Logotherapy* 20, no. 2 (1997): 85–94.

Wong, P. T. "Towards an Integrative Model of Meaning-Centered Counseling and Therapy." *The International Forum for Logotherapy* 22, no. 1 (1999): 48–56.

Wong, P., Meaning Centred Therapy (Toronto: International Society for Existential Psychotherapy, 2007). http://www.meaning.ca/therapy/MCT_articles.htm.

Woznicki, A. *The Transcendant Mystery of Man: A Global Approach to Ecumenism.* Palo Alto, CA: Academica, 2006.

Yanofsky, S. O. *Taking Responsibility and Action: Jewish Education in Vienna* 1918–1938 – *The Austrian State and the Jewish Community of Vienna Balancing the Challenges of Jewish Education in Interwar Vienna.* (2010).

Yalom, Irvin. *Existential Psychotherapy.* New York: Basic Books, 1980.

Yoder, J. D. "Logotherapy as Homecoming." *The International Forum for Logotherapy* 12, no 2 (1989): 74–81.

Yoder, J. "Paradoxical Intention: The Case of Ron." *The International Forum for Logotherapy* 17, no. 2 (1994): 108–113.

Index

About the Author

Dr. Neil Soggie is the author of many books in the areas of Philosophy, History, Religion, and Psychology.

Dr. Soggie is a professional member of the American Counseling Association. He currently serves as the Coordinator for Graduate Counseling Programs at Briercrest College in Canada.

www.ingramcontent.com/pod-product-compliance
Ingram Content Group UK Ltd.
Pitfield, Milton Keynes, MK11 3LW, UK
UKHW012042150926
475560UK00001B/155

9 781442 252080